AN ART OF LIVING

André Maurois

Preface and Translation by

Sergio E. Serrano, Ph.D.

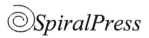 *SpiralPress*

Ambler, Pennsylvania

Original Title:
UN ART DE VIVRE
André Maurois (1885 - 1967)
Librairie Plon, Paris, France, 1939

Published by **SpiralPress**, a division of *HydroScience Inc.*

SpiralPress
1217 Charter Lane
Ambler, PA 19002
Email: hydroscience@earthlink.net
http://home.earthlink.net/~hydroscience
SAN 299-3074

Library of Congress Cataloging-in-Publication Data

Maurois, André, 1885-1967.
[Art de vivre. English]
An art of living / André Maurois.
p. cm.
ISBN 978-0-9655643-5-9 (pbk. : alk. paper)
1. Conduct of life. I. Title.
BJ1582.M34 2007
170'.44--dc22
2007033414

Printed in the United States of America

ISBN: 978-0-9655643-5-9

CONTENTS

iv

PREFACE

"An Art of Living." Do these words evoke the same image to you as they do to me? Our lives are works of art, expressions of inner beauty, conceived and created by our inner selves, tested by the circumstances and experiences of life, perfected and modified by the learning and growing resulting from these experiences. Few authors have expressed these timeless principles with more eloquence than André Maurois (1885 - 1967), one of the most celebrated and prolific French writers of the twentieth century. A biographer, novelist, essayist, and children's writer, Maurois is best known for his vivid, romantic style biographies of such personalities as Shelley, Byron, Balzac, Proust, Chopin, Eisenhower, Franklin, Washington, and many others. As a biographer Maurois is considered unsurpassed. He used dialogue, expressions of interior thought and other techniques that made his biographies easy to read as novels[1]. His style is warm, human, and reflects a profound understanding of history and of human psyche.

An Art of Living was first published in France in 1939. An English translation by James Whitall was published in 1940 and it has been out of print for a long time. The English edition excluded some material of the original French version and added some other writings

---

[1]Kolbert, J., 1985. The Worlds of André Maurois. Susquehanna University Press.

by Maurois.

Now, how is it that a university professor of science and engineering embarks upon a new translation of *An Art of Living*? This book has had a great impact on my life; it positively influenced me in many ways to the point that I feel compelled to bring it back to life hoping it will do the same for you. My first exposure to *An Art of Living* was facilitated by my father. I was an impetuous and idealistic adolescent growing up during tumultuous times in Bogotá, Colombia. My father lent me a copy of the Spanish translation, while indicating to me that he believed this book would help me understand and answer life's most pressing questions. The reading of this book far exceeded this expectation. It captured my heart to the point that I found myself reading over and over excerpts from the various chapters that seemed most relevant at that time, such as *The Art of Loving* and the most beautiful *Open Letter to the Youth*. As any adolescent, I was concerned about love relationships, about attracting the right and compatible partner, about cultivating and protecting a lasting loving relationship.

"Behind the tight rows of women too easily offered, search for those virtuous souls who hesitate before revealing their sweetness and before giving their confidence." (Open Letter to the Youth).

I learned to place in proper perspective courtship and flirting.

"If the partner is unworthy of this confidence, it is necessary to occasionally administer homeopathic dosages of flirting." (The Art of Loving).

I learned about the principles of cultivating a close and profoundly fulfilling relationship. A relationship is an evolving work of art, which must be developed and preserved.

"Old age does not change one in this respect. A beautiful face ages gracefully and it is a joy to find beneath white hair the look and the smile that one once loved beneath dark or blond hair." (The Art of Loving).

Modern relationships seem to confuse love with sexual compatibility, or at least attach them to purely utilitarian restrictions. Today couples split at the first signs of trouble without much effort given towards working through their differences. Love, says Maurois, truly begins after the first wave of initial attraction has passed. The couple must work to build it. Overcoming differences and minimizing the importance of the unavoidable small arguments and petty events constitute a key element. In a loving relationship each partner grows, helps and supports each other through the different stages of life. The reward is a profound intimacy that mellows and refines with time, like the best wine. I thought this was a goal worth pursuing.

After many moves through several countries, one day I regretfully found I had lost the leather-bound copy of *An Art of Living* my father gave me with his own annotations. My second exposure to *An Art of Living* occurred several years later. I was then a young civil engineer, fresh out of college in my twenties, working for the Geological Survey doing groundwater exploration in very inhospitable and remote geographical locations, such as the Amazon basin, and the Northern desertic zones of Colombia. Harsh conditions and isolation were balanced by the company of Maurois' book which, through time and space, provided comfort, guidance, and meaning. Indeed, cherished authors are friends who may give invaluable advice in times of difficulty or during productive solitude. Now the chapters on *The Art of Working* and *The Art of Leadership* took on a very important role. I found many ideas about work self-discipline, and the character and features I should try to emulate in leading workers under extremely adverse environmental and labor conditions. After all, Maurois was not only an erudite scholar of history and a sharp observer of human nature, but also a person who fought in two world wars. Is anyone more qualified to give advice?

"Nothing is so discouraging to subordinates as an indecisive and hesitant chief." (The Art of Leadership).

"Another form of patience is constancy of effort. When an objective is achieved, the true leader does not believe that his affairs and those of his country have been put in order for eternity. Nothing in this world is ever permanently solved." (The Art of Leadership).

I identified with the values in Maurois' writing; many were informally introduced in the bosom of my early family upbringing. The book provided a solid conceptual framework that years later helped me when faced with the harsh realities of life and many stormy battles. Today, one is constantly pressed to react instantly and without much reflection; on the contrary, one should never make an important decision without proper knowledge of all the facts, and without a time to meditate and think about consequences. The importance of maintaining good moral and working relationships between coworkers, the need to control rumors and wasteful gossiping, the necessity of loyalty and faith in the leader, and the support and encouragements of subordinates by the leader are but examples of valuable principles. Loyalty, professional ethics, and integrity are principles with insufficient emphasis today. The deterioration of motivation and productivity in today's corporate world is attributed to the lack of observance of these values.

Then there came the years of graduate school in Canada, particularly those during my doctorate, when *An Art of Living* took on an important role via the chapters on *The Art of Thinking* and *The Art of Working*. In a continent where "multi-tasking" appeared to be the desired mode of operation, I learned that, on the contrary, one must pinpoint a very specific topic of work and drop everything else in order to devote all energies to accomplishing the set task.

"Amicable men are those who are interested in everything; men who accomplish things, who finish their tasks, are those who, during a given period of time interest themselves in one thing only. In America these men are said to possess "single-track minds;" their tenacity and their obsession are sometimes fastidious; their repeated attacks end with demolishing all obstacles to success." (The Art of Working).

While writing my doctoral dissertation, *An Art of Living* helped me recognize the limitations of logic to create something new.

"Logic cannot invent anything. It is condemned to eternally reiterate that A is A. If it adds anything, this new notion must be borrowed either from experience or intuition, both of which are outside the range of logic... Logic has certainly given speed to the spirit; it has provided it with an agility it lacked, but also with the dangerous habit of believing that all is accomplished when it has made a reasoning which has the appearance of truth." (The Art of Thinking).

Maurois accurately predicted the insufficiency and limitations of the scientific method to solve society's most pressing problems. He also anticipated the over reliance on the scientific method. Indeed, even the most descriptive fields of study, such as sociology, exhibit today an over emphasis in quantitative methods. As a scientist and an engineer, I recognize the importance of the scientific method to generate new knowledge and technological progress. Yet, experimentation and abstract reasoning did not always provide me with a solution to technical problems after many attempts and trials. Maurois pointed me in the right direction: the use of intuition, creativity, the study and adaptation of past experience of other researchers. The balance between the logic of science and the qualitative attributes of mind led me to success many times.

"Then, it is important that reason recognize its mistakes, regain contact with reality, and renouncing the idle notions condemned by experience suggest new hypotheses. It is only by means of the constant collaboration between reason, experience, and action that we can achieve —not

a permanent victory, because such is not in the nature of things, but a moment of respite and repose underneath one of those fragile shelters which we call civilizations." (The Art of Thinking).

An Art of Living was also a companion during my years teaching and doing research at the University of Waterloo, the University of Kentucky, and Temple University. In today's academic system, a faculty is given tenure and promotion if, among other things, he demonstrates he is a good teacher. To measure the quality of teaching, institutions rely almost exclusively on quantitative methods in the form of the student's evaluation of faculty teaching. Once again, we see an over reliance on quantitative methods, but most importantly, can the students judge a teacher independently of their feelings for the faculty, their like or dislike of the subject, and the requirements of work? The result has been a generation of teachers and professors that spend more time entertaining and pleasing the students than making them work and learn. However, Maurois foresaw and warned us of the dangers of such an education:

"To amuse is not to teach. The object of teaching is to erect a framework of elemental knowledge in a child's mind and gradually to raise the child to the level of adults in his time. Later in life, the facts taught by experience and new discoveries will add themselves to this framework. It is senseless to attempt to alter this natural order and to appeal to a child's mind by entertaining him with the spectacle of modern life. . .That which has been learned without effort is easily forgotten. For the same reason, oral instruction which does not require any personal

participation from the student is always rather useless. Eloquence slides in and out of young minds. To listen is not to work." (The Art of Working).

Maurois was quite correct in distrusting an education too geared towards the use of audio visual aids. While technology certainly facilitates the illustration of facts and reference material, it should not replace the students' efforts to investigate, read, write, and assimilate certain topics. Copying essays from the Internet is usually done without the material going through the student's brain, and raises other questions about intellectual property. There is also the problem of overloading the curricula with too much information, but of very shallow depth.

"*It is better to teach a few things perfectly than many things haphazardly. It is absolutely useless to overload the curriculum. The object of education is not to produce technicians, but good spirits.*" (The Art of Working).

Lately, the chapter on the *Art of Growing Old* has taken on a new dimension. It is helping me rekindle some of my hobbies and plan for a productive and enjoyable retirement.

"*I have encountered several old men who were like the wise men of our dreams. Released not only from the frenzies of love, but also from the responsibilities of a long-term future, they do not envy young people; they feel compassionate about the young ones because they still have to overcome the stormy sea of existence. Deprived of a few pleasures which they barely miss, they keenly enjoy those that remain. They know how useless advice can be and realize that everyone must live his own life. We are glad to listen to their recollections because they spare us their criticism, and when things become too difficult, we even ask them to resume their leadership. This we do it more readily because everyone knows that they do not wish this power."* (The Art of Growing Old).

There is so much insight in this book! Maurois accurately predicts the ultimate failure of all social revolutions; the necessity of slow change in human customs and attitudes as a key to lasting changes; the technological development and implementation of robots in large assembly lines; the characteristics of a reasonable and effective government; and the inner virtues to cultivate in order to successfully overcome the adversities of life. I have come to realize that in the mist of the constant changes in my life, *An Art of Living* has been one of the few constants. As a science educator, I strive to give my students, not just an enumeration of facts and logical exercises, but also a balanced exposure to professional ethics and life values. I constantly mention Maurois' *An Art of Living*, only to find that those interested students who follow my advice to read it, complain about the difficulty of finding an out-of-print English translation, which does not have the same contents and style as the original French edition. Why a book that is as relevant today as it was last century, as useful to the youth and adult alike, as timeless and profound in its principles, has not been reprinted eludes me. I recently realized that perhaps it was my duty to put aside my science writing for a while and devote some time to call the attention of English readers to this beautiful, yet forgotten, book.

This new limited edition is the response to that call. A few remarks about the present translation are in order. The first one is that I have endeavored to remain as close as possible to the original French edition. In achieving this, I have translated each sentence in a way that emulates, as faithfully as possible, Maurois writing style. This presented important challenges as to the translation of many beautiful and poetic French paragraphs into English, resulting at times in sentences that look unusually long. As a science and technical writer, I recognize the importance of conciseness and clarity. English-writing style today appears dominated by a trend to brevity. Yet, this is not a technical manual nor a typical English monograph. I submitted this issue for discussion to my students. Two schools of opinion emerged: those in favor of respecting the original French writing style of the author, and those in favor of "editing" each sentence to make it more appealing and "to the point" to modern English readers in America. I believe the latter would neglect the poetic contents of the book. The real benefit of *An Art of Living*, as well as of many classical books in any language, is that the sentences are not merely a collection of words to convey a practical thought, but a communication to the spirit of the reader. Maurois speaks to the soul of the reader. For these reasons, this translation attempts to respect not only the meaning intended by the writer, but also his style.

Another remark relates to the translation of words that have become politically incorrect with the times. This refers for instance to using "he" when referring to both men and women. This issue was heatedly discussed by my students. Again, there were two schools of thought: those in support of an edition that respects the sensitivities of certain groups, and those that demand that a translation respects the style of the author. In the end, I sided with the latter and remained as close as possible to the author's writing. I believe each author writes within the cultural context of his or her time, as Maurois did. Although I firmly believe in gender inclusiveness in writing, I decided not to make any changes in his writing style. The same could be said about a book that makes references to items, places, or personages that may appear unfamiliar to the intended reader of a new translation. Once again, this edition attempts an accurate translation of the author's meaning. For instance, I do not believe the word "Café" should be translated into "Bar" in order to make it more understandable to the intended readership. In my opinion, if the American public does not understand the meaning, atmosphere, and ambiance of a Café, then it really ought to; although I believe that American society is slowly embracing many foreign customs, such as the benefits of slow and engaging conversation at a Café.

Besides attempting to reproduce Maurois style and meaning, this edition remains faithful to the original French version in regards to contents. In other words, many passages that were omitted in the 1940's translation are included in the present one, in particular the beautiful *Open Letter to the Youth*. This contains sound advice that touched me when I was very young and I feel it has an equal value for today's youth. Its content was as valid and relevant in 1939 as it is today, as we attempt to define meaningful changes in the 21st century. The *Letter*, as well as the rest of this treasure book, contains timeless advice on the various important aspects of life: love relationships, work and career, leadership, aging, and retirement. This is not a "self-help" book with precise recipes for life. It feels as if a very wise person is talking to you in a simple way, giving sound advice and much common sense. It lets the reader think by himself to find his own meaning, her own truth. There is a strong value for personal and professional ethics and every concept is presented with many references to other writers, anecdotes, and quotations. Many passages use beautiful metaphors to emphasize a principle that only an erudite in the history of humanity can provide.

Thus, here is a tribute to André Maurois, and a gift to my students and the public. I suggest you read it slowly, not more than one section at a time. If possible, find a solitary place where you will not be disturbed for at least half an hour; turn off your cell phone, sit in a comfortable chair, and read it in a soft voice to enhance contemplation. In a world where the information revolution controls our lives, the visual and audio over stimulation numb our minds, and the worries, stresses, and disputes ruin our nerves, you can find solace by rediscovering the joys of reading a wise master, a friend.

Sergio E. Serrano, Ph.D.
Philadelphia, May 2007

I
THE ART OF THINKING

1. — THE WORLD AND THE WORLD OF THINKING

I turn my eyes towards my study window. For a moment my thoughts mingle with the images which seem to be painted on the glass. Beyond the geometric pattern of the balcony railing, I see the green waves of the woods washed in the faint bluish mist of the Parisian mornings. At the horizon rises a line of hills and at the pinnacle of Mont Valerien, whose skirts are clothed with dark trees, a hospital reminds of a Florentine convent encircled by black cypresses. Squadrons of swallows pass across the pale sky thinly veiled by clouds. Far off toward Versailles, airplanes are wheeling and snoring. They call up memories of war, aerial bombardments, and sirens groaning in the night. I cease contemplating the green foliage and the singing of birds. I think about the death of a civilization, about the end of the Roman Empire, about a little town on the Algerian coast which seemed prosperous and charming around the third century A.C., and nothing but a tragic empty ruin a hundred years later. I think how the ruins of our capitals would look like one day.

Thus, my daydream concerns not only the present

aspects of the universe, but contains visions of distant lands, recounts ancient happenings, and evolves theories of an unpredictable future. It is as if my spirit were a private world in which is reflected the huge exterior universe without limits of time or space. Philosophers have sometimes called this reduced model of the universe a *microcosm,* and *macrocosm* the immense world we live in and would like to understand and transform. "The mind, like an angel," wrote an alchemist in the Middle Ages, "takes possession of all things that are included in the macrocosm." Let us rather say that the mind *tries* to take possession of all things and that the world is reflected on us, distorted like the sky and the flowers in a silver garden ball.

The cause of the extreme confusion of this daydream is that everything here, the mirror as well as the objects, the microcosms as well as the macrocosm, are perpetually moving. Indeed, there is before me an image that seems more or less clear: the iron railing, the foliage of the trees, the birds, and the hills at the horizon, which are here and now. But all memory, anticipation, and reasoning oscillates according to the rhythm of the waves of the sea within us. My ignorance, my passions, my errors, and my forgetfulness cause distortion, even though everything continually changes into new and strange forms. In our minds the vast world is like a map with blurry contours and moving lines, which we must nevertheless use constantly to choose a direction.

The desire to think clearly should impose a long wait and an endless search on us, but the need to act is urgent. The health of one of our children is failing. What is his sickness? Is it physical or mental? Whom should we consult? Is medicine of any use? Is it a true science? What is a science? To study these questions seriously a lifetime would be required, but what can we do? We must find the answer why our patient is dying. There is not enough time for an exploration of the outside world. The only view of it immediately at our disposal is the tiny confused one which our mind offers.

We call thinking the effort we make to guess or foresee, by combining symbols and images, the consequences our actions will have on real things. All thinking is the sketching out of an action. According to this sketch the picture of our life will be painted, not without corrections. In order to act correctly, we must make an effort to think correctly, according to Pascal. What is correct thinking? It is to make our little interior model of the outside world as exact as possible. If the laws of our microcosm coincide closely with those of the macrocosm, if our map represents with relative precision the country through which we must journey, then there is some possibility that our actions may be adjusted to our needs, our desires, or our fears.

Are there methods that permit man to control his thoughts so that his subsequent actions will fit easily into the existing scheme of things? Is it possible to draw a true map of the universe, navigate with this map, towards definite ends, and to reach a chosen port? Such is our topic.

2. — THINKING WITH THE BODY

It seems that the thoughts best adapted to the universe of things are those recorded upon living bodies in the form of instincts or habits. A cat leaps upon a table covered with objects. It stands there gracefully and effortlessly, without breaking a cup, without breaking a vase. Such a series of movements implies a careful calculation of the strength required and an exact choice of the spot to land upon. But neither the choice nor the calculation was conscious. The cat has thought with its muscles and its eyes. Throughout a present sight it has imagined the future movements of its body, and these images of movement have in their turn evoked the positions to be taken by its feet, its back, and its head.

In the same manner a tennis player, a football player, a fencer, or an acrobat thinks with his body. The fencer never has time to say to himself: "Here my opponent makes a double feint and then breaks; I am going to answer him with a double stop and an attack in depth." He thinks with his foil and his fingers. As a boy, I practiced the gymnastics. I knew that I could not practice a routine with the fixed bar or the parallel bars unless I imagined it with perfect precision. If I could imagine my body balanced in the air, if I could measure in advance the extent of its wavering, if during this anticipatory thinking I could choose the fraction of a second in which my biceps had to be contracted or my legs raised to accelerate the motion, then everything became easy as though by a miracle. But if there was the tiniest break in this imaginary film, if it was out of focus for a few millimeters, then the rhythm broke down and the exercise seemed impossible.

It is not by a process of reasoning that the sculptor decides to change the curve of a hip. A direct communication has been established between his eyes fixed on the model and his fingers caressing the statue. Like the gymnast, the good worker and the artist think with their bodies. Some living things learn to think with the bodies of others. An animal in a horde thinks with the herd. If panic seizes a flock of sheep, each animal runs with the flock, not because it knows and understands the reason for the panic, but because the experience of the species, engraved in fundamental instincts, teaches that if a sheep does not follow the flock it will be at the mercy of its enemies. Like those animals, people living in native indigenous cultures close to nature, children, and crowds are extremely susceptible to instinctive and corporeal thinking.

Traveling on a steamer, I once encountered a boy of four or five years of age crossing the Atlantic alone. He had been entrusted to the captain. The boy's intuition surpassed that of any adult when guessing the passengers who liked him, and those who were annoyed by him. He loved the friendly ones and avoided the others. Undoubtedly he was guided by signs which to us would have been imperceptible. After a quarrel, two lovers are not reconciled by words; a sigh suddenly produces a smile, their eyes meet, and their bodies draw together. Soon they are in each other's arms, far more certain of an agreement than if a long talk had calmed them.

3. — THINKING WITH WORDS

There seems to be a corporeal thinking which guides some of our actions with marvelous security. But its range is short. The mole thinks very satisfactorily with its feet, but it cannot think farther than its feet. It knows nothing of the many ugly molehills that are formed in a green lawn, nor does it realize the rage of the gardener or the unpleasant consequences of this frenzy for the race of moles. An aviator has precise reflexes which guide him to make safe landings. But certainly the hands of the aviator had nothing to do with inventing the airplane.   The national leader who administers the finances of a country cannot think with his body. He cannot even think, as the gymnast does, by means of mental pictures of actions, because these pictures would be too numerous. If the duty is to improve the economic situation of millions of people, the statesman cannot think, "I am working for this merchant or that farmer I have met, or f or that jobless man whose difficulties I am aware of." In order to speed up its thinking, the financial leader must replace these pictures of human beings, fields, houses, and industries by symbols and signs representing either a man or a thing, or all men belonging to a certain class, and these symbols are words.

The workman, juggler, or gymnast who thinks with his hands manipulates objects which have weight and resistance: bricks, balls, or his own body. The man who thinks with words manipulates only sounds or symbols. This makes any action singularly easy. You are at a hotel in the morning; you lift the telephone and pronounce the word "tea." In a few moments you are miraculously brought a cup, a saucer, a spoon, bread, milk, marmalade, a pot of tea, and hot water. Imagine the complexity of real actions that required the production of these things for you. Imagine the Chinese farmers growing and harvesting the tea; the English steamer transporting them; the captain and his crew fighting a typhoon; the Perigord cowboy driving his beasts to pasture, milking them; the engineer of the train carrying the milk; the baker kneading the bread; the Spanish or Provençal girls picking the oranges for the marmalade . . . One spoken syllable has put all these people at your service.

The man who thinks with his hands has a limited effect upon the universe. He acts only upon what he touches. The man who thinks with words can, without effort, set peoples, armies, and continents in motion. How about the head of a government pronouncing the word "mobilization" and with this tiny act, requiring of him nothing more than an imperceptible movement of the lips, he will drag all the reservists in Europe from their homes and families; he will fill the sky with bombers that will destroy ancient villages; he will bring about the destruction of a world and the end of a civilization. When one reflects upon the possible effects of a single word, one understands why language was regarded as having a magic power by primitive peoples. Kipling's Hindoos searched for the "master word" that would give them power over people and things. Faust browsed through the old books of the alchemists for formulas to evoke or drive away spirits. In the Arabian Nights "Sesame" opened a door. This was a legend but a true one. In all societies there are words that open doors and words that evoke evil spirits. Every speaker earns his dinner with some "Sesame"; every riot is generated by a master word.

The man who thinks with his hands moves heavy objects and moves them slowly, brick after brick, step by step. His care is assured by the very difficulty of his actions. He is obliged to maintain this correspondence between the exterior and interior world, which we have established as a warranty of true thinking, for if he does not do so the bricks will bruise his hands, he will mishandle the balls he is juggling, or he will fall from the parallel bars at the gymnasium. But actions are too easy for the man who thinks with words. The interval between error and punishment is too long for him to realize his responsibilities. He plays with tenuous symbols and forgets the terrible consequences that may follow. He is tempted to take, as Leibnitz said, "the straw of words for the grain of things," and to believe that everything has been done when only words have been pronounced.

The difficulty is that things resist. One can say everything with words. Napoleon III said: "The principle of nationalities must be respected." And this abstract phrase, which could be taken for the truth because it evoked no precise image, has brought about the destruction of modern Europe. An economist, sitting at his desk, writes: "To increase salaries is to increase the purchasing power and therefore to put an end to the crisis." These words were as good as many others. They had a flavor of truth and the economist pronounces them in good faith. In fact, the measures these words inspired did not end the economic disorder. Why? Because the microcosm could not influence the macrocosm; because there was a divergence between words and things; because the simplicity of this phrase did not represent precisely the complexity of the situation.

4. — LOGIC AND REASONING

It would be a dangerous and a terrible thing if, in order to judge of the value of a phrase or a formula, one had to wait for its good or evil consequences. It is natural that, from the beginning of civilization, wise men had searched for a surer method of handling these explosive symbols with preventive skills. In the manner of present-day traffic regulation, men have tried to regulate the circulation of words. This is what later was called logic. Logic should be the art of following, in the handling of words, certain rules that would also give assurances, because these rules of the interior world would coincide with those of the exterior world. What we call the laws of human reason are some rules for thinking, which would be valid for all men in every age. Some of them are evident, for example the principle of non-contradiction: a thing cannot be both itself and its opposite. Not everything can be said; one cannot say simultaneously: "Two and two are four" and "Two and two are five"; it cannot be said: "This dress is white" and

"This dress is black"; or "I want this country to be free" and "I want it to be enslaved." For a long time humanity has waited for a kind of grammar of thinking that would discard error based upon fundamental principles. This logic, which was Aristotle's, and in the Middle Ages adopted by the Scholastic Philosophers, is a discipline not to be neglected. It shelters our reasoning from certain errors, but it is insufficient to constitute an art of thinking, for the following reasons:

Logic cannot invent anything. It is condemned to eternally reiterate that A is A. If it adds anything, this new notion must be borrowed either from experience or intuition, both of which are outside the range of logic. Logic allows one to say: "This dress is a dress," but only experience permits one to add that the dress is fragile or that it is wrinkled. Kant has done away with the folly of conceiving pure reason ever to get on without experience: "In its passion to enlarge its knowledge, reason, made confident by this proof of its power, believes it sees the extent of infinity opening before it. *The fleet-winged dove, rapidly cleaving the air and feeling its resistance, thinks it would fly much better in a vacuum...* Thus Plato, neglecting the physical world which keeps reason within such narrow limits, ventures beyond into the empty spaces of pure understanding. He does not realize that, in spite of his efforts, he is making no progress; he lacks the support necessary to sustain him, from which his understanding may be set in motion." A large number of our political reformers flutter about vainly in the empty spaces of pure understanding.

Logic has certainly given speed to the spirit; it has provided it with an agility it lacked, but also with the dangerous habit of believing that all is accomplished when it has made a reasoning which has the appearance of truth. But history of philosophical doctrine shows that, in the course of centuries, men have been able to prove almost everything. They have been able to prove the truth of contradictory philosophies and then their falsity; they have been able to prove the necessity for democracy and also its impossibility; they have been able to prove both the separateness of races and their confusion. "All proofs," said the philosopher Alain, "are for me clearly discredited." In essence, *everything can be proven if the words employed are not clearly defined.*

A demonstration in algebra is irrefutable because each term is defined in such a precise manner that the demonstrator can say nothing that is beyond of what the audience understands. Identities in logic are true identities. But the words used in speaking abut emotions, about the conduct of government, about the economy, are vague words which may be employed in the same argument with several different meanings. To reason with a poor language is like using a pair of scales with inaccurate weights.

5. — THE CARTESIAN METHOD

The Cartesian method is an attempt to eliminate certain errors from such reasoning. "I had a strong desire," said Descartes, "to learn to distinguish the true from the false, in order that I might act with a clear vision and go through life with confidence." We must remember the illustrious rules that constituted his art of thinking. The first one: *not to accept anything as true unless it is evidently recognized as such.* This rule may seem too simple. "Why," you ask, "would I accept a thing as true if I do not believe it is so?" Descartes replies to your question by laying down another rule: *carefully avoid haste and prejudice.*

Haste is to be avoided because man cannot understand difficult things quickly. The student who skips through the pages of the textbook will never learn geometry. But human beings are usually in a hurry. Some are because of necessity. They must take an examination on a certain day and a whole field in science or the history of a whole period must be studied before that day arrives. The expert has promised to hand in his report by a given deadline; the government waits; if the expert delays too much, politicians will make some arbitrary decision; an incomplete report is better than none at all. The journalist would want to have just a few more hours in which to consider a new and obscure question, but the printers are already demanding his column, so that the paper will not miss the 2:00 A.M. train. The action demands a deadline.

Others are in a hurry because of their vanity. They hate to admit ignorance of anything. A specialist thinks himself disgraced if he has to reply: "I will look into this." Look at how in government, in society, and in business meetings, people speak authoritatively upon questions with which they are unfamiliar. Someone will talk about Czechoslovakia, about Ethiopia, about Hungary without ever having been there or even having studied its history and customs. Another will give an unfavorable opinion of our aviation when what he knows about it has come from rumors and from unproven statements. Still another will tear a woman's reputation in bits by telling false stories of her private life. The average value of conversations could be significantly improved by the constant use of four simple words: "I do not know," or even better of Louis XIV's favorite remark: "I shall see." If we swear never to let ourselves be forced to make a precipitous decision, and never to be hurried into forming rash judgments ourselves, we will have taken an important step towards Cartesian wisdom.

Haste is not the only cause of error; there is also prejudice. We are not like flat mirrors, but like deforming ones. We approach questions, not like virgin transparent surfaces, but with family and group opinions already formed; our nature, our hereditary disposition, and our education impose prejudiced "feelings" on us. Do you wish to calculate the effect your lineage has upon your thinking? Try to recall your successive opinions about Clemenceau, Caillaux, and Daladier after reading articles for and against them in your newspapers; you hated or adored them with good faith but not with good sense.

Our self interest is another cause of prejudice. Pascal said that if geometry stirred our emotions as much as politics we would not be able to analyze it so well. There are very few men who do not reckon the cost to themselves of a new system of taxes before approving it. Imagine a doctor who, based on a theory, has built up a method of treatment which would make him wealthy and famous. Suppose he discovers that his method is based upon a false theory. Don't you think his mind would suggest to him a thousand good reasons for doubting the validity of the objections to the theory?

Everything that is in agreement with our personal desires seems true; everything that is not enrages us. Consider the political life of Chateaubriand. During his exile he became, owing to the French Revolution, an English style constitutional monarchist. After the Restoration, Louis XVIII endeavored to give France such type of a government. If Chateaubriand had not surrendered to his personal feelings, he would have wholeheartedly supported the king's efforts, but he was irritated at not being the one chosen to direct the new government. Because he was unfairly treated, he developed a violent hostility against the king, against Decazes, and later against Villèle, and he opposed his own doctrine with arguments which seemed admirable because of his gift of language but which were in fact detestable. There is no absurdity or contradiction in which a man could not fall because of his passions. When love or hate takes control, reason must submit and then discover justifications for his folly. Once again: "Every proof is clearly dishonorable to us," because everything can be proven if we so desire it with passion.

Some people believe themselves to be independent of their environments or of their countries because the circumstances of their lives have inspired feelings of rebellion. But rebellion is not a guarantee of independence. On the contrary it is sometimes an acute form of prejudice. The writer who has been abused during childhood will put himself forward as a free thinker in his attacks to religion and family life, but his revolt is the revolt of a slave. The expatriate believes he is demonstrating his freedom when he criticizes the tyrant. But is he qualified to judge the regime of a country who has mistreated him? Descartes would not have thought so. Some think with the clan; others think against the clan. They are different, but equivalent, forms of prejudice.

The author of *The Discourse on Method* first advises us to keep our reason free from passion, and then to make good use of it. For this purpose he provides several rules: "*Organize your thoughts in regular order, from the simplest to the most complex. . . Divide problems into as many parts as possible. . . Make your enumerations so complete and your surveys so general that you may be certain of omitting nothing.*" This method has undoubtedly been of extraordinary service, first to Descartes himself, and then to the scholars of his day who later went far in mathematics, mechanics, astronomy, and in some branches of physics. The Cartesian method is still marvelously effective whenever it is a question for the mind, either about discovering its own laws, as in mathematics, or about studying the phenomena which abstraction or remoteness has simplified (as it happens in astronomy). It has appeared not useless but insufficient when applied to the more complex sciences.

In many branches of physics, in chemistry, biology, medicine, economics, politics, the Cartesian method, though still a necessary check, it does not make it possible the solution of problems, and it is not sufficient to direct our actions. How is one "to conduct one's thoughts in regular order" when *time* is the main factor? How is one to "omit nothing" when the variables affecting the problem are countless? The method constructs within us a microcosm of glass and steel whose exquisitely cut gears engage with perfect precision, but we know very well that the exterior world is not fashioned in the image of this exact and transparent mechanism. The windblown leaves, the storm-driven clouds, the works in the fields, and the passions of the city have no place here.

6. — THE EXPERIMENTAL METHOD

Based on an apple seed, there is no reasoning, however well conducted and free from haste and prejudice, that would enable us to foretell what the shape of the tree or the flavor of its fruit will be. In regards to an unknown microbe, no syllogism or theory would give us power to describe the disease that may attack a patient inoculated with it. It is not to our spirit, but to nature, to the world of things, that such questions must be posed. The method which, for two centuries has given men such amazing power over the external world is a blending of logic, observation and experimentation. Reasoning is a part of the method, but its conclusions will always be confronted by facts, accepted if they are confirmed by these facts, and cast aside mercilessly if they contradict the conclusions.

The experimental method is often attributed to Bacon. He may have been the first to formulate its principles clearly, but it was employed unconsciously since the remotest antiquity. The primitive man practiced experimentation, just like Monsieur Jordain produced prose: unknowingly. Each one of us makes several experiments every day. This morning my study is infested by wasps. I try to discover what attracts them. Perhaps are these carnations on my table, and their fragrance? At random, I remove the flowers and in a few moments the wasps disappear. Verification: I bring the carnations from the adjoining room and put them back on my table; the wasps reappear. I have discovered one of the laws of nature. I will request that flowers no longer be put on my table at this time of the year.

Reduced to its essential elements, the experimental method is a fairly simple one. It consists, according to Claude Bernard, "of systematically testing our ideas with facts." Man's observations suggest to him hypothescs about the relationships between phenomena. In order to verify these hypotheses, scholars make further and more rigorous observations. "The observer," says Cuvier, "listens to nature; the experimenter questions her and obliges her to reveal herself." For example, he varies the cause and notes the variation in the effect. If he discovers a fixed relationship between cause and effect, the idea of such linkage is then confirmed. Nevertheless, error is possible. "Following this, then because of this" is frequently a false axiom. That a war breaks out after an eclipse does not prove that the eclipse caused it. There is the story of the Oxford student who drank numerous whiskies and sodas every afternoon and then he could not think clearly. He gave up whisky and took brandy and soda, then gin with his soda, but the still ended up drunk. "Undoubtedly," he concluded, "it is the soda." If he had been a wiser experimenter, he would have gone farther and tried a confirming test; by eliminating the soda and keeping the whisky, brandy, and gin he would have discovered his error.

The scholar is a man who, by means of observations and experiments, he draws hypotheses about the constant relationships between phenomena. If his hypotheses are verified by every conceivable experiment, he regards them provisionally as laws of nature. Every time I let go of an object I am holding, it falls. The velocity of its falling can be calculated and the acceleration of its falling toward a given spot is constant. We therefore admit the existence of laws regarding the falling of objects. Science, which is the sum of such observations, does not constitute in anyway an explanation of the universe; it is merely, as Valéry says, "a collection of recipes that have given good results." But these recipes might fail. If in this instance I let go of the book I am now holding, and if, instead of falling, it should rise to the ceiling, I would be surprised, but science would not be affected. Science would merely be obliged to find a more complex law to account for this phenomenon.

Experimental science assumes but one metaphysical hypothesis, which is the permanency of the laws of nature. If we do not believe in nature's obedience, or seeming obedience, to fixed laws, it would be obviously absurd to observe phenomena. If water at the same pressure started to boil one day at fifty degrees Celcius, another at seventy five, and another at one hundred without our being able to find any way of predicting these variations, it would be useless to study physics. Happily this is not the case. Phenomena have a curious constancy. Why? The philosopher, the theologian, and even the mathematician has some ideas about the matter. The experimenter knows nothing about it, and on the other hand, why should he care? He concludes that the method consists in observing phenomena, deriving hypotheses f rom these obscrvations, verifying these hypotheses by experiment, abandoning them if they cannot be verified, and regulating our conduct according to seemingly stable laws. This method which, as Bacon said, commands nature while obeying her, has produced amazing results.

Owing to its ability to establish constant relations between certain phenomena, which can be easily produced by human forces, and certain others which require more than human force, if one wishes to produce them directly, the experimental method enables man to become infinitely more powerful than man. When a child sets all the mechanisms at an exposition in motion by pressing a button, the action is symbolic of the power which science puts at the disposal of the weakest of human creatures. Astonishing power! It is admirable that a tiny insect cast into the universe upon a speck of mud has succeeded, not only in measuring the distance from his own speck to others like it, but in changing its climate, its vegetation, and its animals within a few years. It is admirable that he has come to build machines capable of carrying him around his globe in a few hours. It is admirable that he has come to conquer cold, darkness, and famine.

But let us say it once again: The scientific method does not explain the universe; it will never explain it, but considering the power it has given to men over physical, chemical, and biological phenomena, it is natural that many have asked themselves: "Why should not an art of thinking, which has succeeded so well with the physical world, be applied to the life in human societies? Why should not the method, which has made possible the construction of immense factories where robots of steel and copper do the work of men, be used also to bring happiness to those who have been replaced by the machines? Why should not the method, which permits the creation of races of animals and varieties of flowers, also permit the creation of the superman?" When his children lost their tempers in a political argument, Lord Salisbury said to them: "Let's try to think this out chemically." By that he meant: "Let us try to regard human elements as we regard chemical ones in an experiment. Let us not be prejudiced in anyway about its results. Let us put the chemicals in the retort, heat them, and observe their reaction. If This reaction proves contrary to our doctrine, we will abandon our doctrine." This would be a political science. Is such a procedure possible? Does science constitute the last word about the art of thinking for men?

7. — THE SHORTCOMINGS OF EXPERIENCE

After several decades of high hopes, at the beginning of which Renan expected to find our world scientifically controlled by members of the Institute, and at the end of which Bertrand Russell imagined that a machine would enable us to know the exact moments of past and future events, we must realize, alas, that the experimental method, after having given us the already described amazing power over the external world, has produced very few good results in the domain of ethical, political, and social life.

It is easy to understand why:

1.- *Experimentation requires a closed system which*

could be artificially isolated . If we wish to know under what conditions water will boil, we isolate a group of elements: source of heat, container, liquid; we apply a given pressure and we succeed in removing most of the exterior influences. Experiments of this kind are not possible if it concerns complex human societies which we cannot detach to isolate in a closed system.

2.- *Experimentation requires that the experiment may be rerun if necessary,* and confirmed by both verification and validation if appropriate. This is difficult in psychology; impossible in sociology. What rational statesman would try to suppress an entire class in a society "to see what would happen?" What communist would agree, in order to conduct an honest verification, to the reestablishment of capitalism?

3.- *Finally, the experimental method requires the good faith and disinterestedness of the experimenter.* These virtues, which are in fact rare when scientific experiments not of the kind to awaken the most violent passions are involved, become superhuman when these passions are aroused.

The scientific search for truth requires that reason shall never cling vehemently to a hypothesis. "If the first duty of a scholar is to invent a system, his second is to regard it with disgust," or at least to be indifferent to it. But man is man and he will not be detached from anything that he believes he has found. Pouchet did not want Pasteur to be right. The physicist who thought he had discovered the N rays did not want to be wrong. It happens that the desire to discover a law may lead the experimenter to tamper unconsciously with his findings in a manner favorable to the discovery. In medicine every specialist believes, often sincerely, that all of his patients are suffering from the disease in which he specializes. The psychiatrist will say to you: "Almost all illnesses are psychological." The endocrinologist will see a disease of the glands where the gastroenterologist will discover only ailments in his own arena.

At least medicine is partly a science. It deals with a specific human body, which in the course of an experiment may be partially isolated. But when the reactions and the passions of millions of human bodies are at play, as it happens in economics and politics, the most contradictory theories, *all of them*, may be supported by facts. One can say with reason that experience has condemned the liberal economy of the nineteenth century since it generated collectivism in our own time; but one can also say that experience has condemned collectivism, because the latter was obliged to maintain or reinstate under new names the more or less classic formulas of private property, in order to save the society it conquered.

Is it possible to draw laws upon such experiments?

.ently not, for what constitutes scientific ⌐_ erimentation is the large number of experiments and the possibility of repeating them. But in economics, each experiment requires the time and the lives of several generations of humans. The so-called Roosevelt experiment and the Blum experiment are merely short phases of political cycles too costly to be set in motion voluntarily, too vast to be observed as a whole, too confusing to offer any educational value to future generations, whose predicament will never be the same.

What is true in economics is also true in politics. We are told: "England has made the democratic experiment and this experiment has been a happy one." But this reasoning is not scientific at all, for other peoples are not the English people. Democracy is only a word beneath which realities must be written, and English realities are neither French, Spanish, nor Italian realities. English democracy implies English political life, the taste for open discussion and compromise, the intensity of local life, the understanding on the part of an open-minded aristocracy for the middle classes whom it consorts with freely, the agreement between Parliament and the "elite" of the land, in short, a constitutional monarchy.

To compare democracy with fascism is to compare two words, not two realities or two precise definitions. Between complete liberty and absolute authority, innumerable types of society are conceivable and in fact realizable. How is one to discover by experiment whether liberty is better than authority, when there is no means of measuring the degree of liberty in a nation? This does not mean that a certain form of liberty is not desirable; it does not mean that there is not a political truth for a nation at a given time, but it does mean that this truth must be discovered by methods *which are not those of science.*

"To think chemically" during political and social problems? It is possible that we need to attempt this, but it must be honestly admitted that this would be impossible in the majority of cases. That is why many men, so reasonable when they speak of their profession, are so unreasonable the moment they begin to discuss general principles. When an electrical system is to be repaired, the little world which represents it in the mind of the engineer constitutes such a precise map that he is perfectly at home amongst the wires and circuits. But when a country is to be reconstructed, there is no chart of its social life by which we can lay a sure course towards progress and happiness. Even if rigorously applied, the experimental method is as powerless as pure reason to guide a statesman, a company executive, or the commander in chief of an army.

And yet these men must nevertheless act, make decisions. What should be the basis of their decisions?

Alain writes, and this is a very profound sentence: "Action must precede volition." We verify this as soon as we act. A puppy thrown into the water will swim even though he has never had any swimming experience before. He swims before he decides to do it. At birth we are all young animals thrown into the sea of things, and we swim as best we can. The writer, beginning work on a novel, has no precise idea of what he wants to write. If he knew it word for word, his novel would already be written. He throws himself into the water. Each chapter suggests the following one. Action precedes volition.

To make plans may be necessary, but the making of plans is not to act. Inside every café and bar, speakers describe admirable plans: "If I were President of the Council . . . If I were Mussolini If I were the Minister of Air Transportation . . ." Drafting a permanent peace treaty? Child's play and Wilson succeeded on the whole in doing it. But to maintain peace in Europe for two years, or two months? A superhuman feat. "Thinking is easy," says Goethe, "acting is difficult, and acting according to our thinking is the most difficult thing in the world." And Tolstoy: "It is easier to produce ten volumes of philosophical writing than to put one principle into practice." In a great number of situations, which are the most important to our existence, we must find our way in a labyrinth of actions without possessing all of the elements of the map. Then, what does the art of thinking become?

8. — THOUGHT AND ACTION

From the beginning of this essay we have shown the infallibility of instinctive thought, but the narrow limits of its domain. The dream of the man of action would be to find once again the security of instinct, but in cases infinitely more complex. In other words, for the man of action the art of thinking is the art of making thought instinctive. *We do not at all mean to say that the man of action should neglect reason.* He should have thought about what he is going to do; he should have envisioned, like the young Bonaparte at Toulon, the problems which he will have to solve one day; he should have observed many facts and derive laws from his observations. But this meditation, these observations, and these laws must be inscribed within his body. It is necessary that thinking reach "the deeper layers and *be possessed with good reflexes.*" For in this way only will he acquire the flashing speed of decision which events almost always require.

Consider an old clinician at the moment when a patient is brought to him. Perhaps, like his colleagues, he will require tests and these tests will assist him in his subconscious reasoning, but his instinct, the result of the thousands of cases he has observed, will dictate his diagnosis. His reasons for feeling anxious or reassured in regard to a patient are so numerous that he will often find it hard to put them into words. Compared to a young and brilliant professor, he will not seem to be very wise. And nevertheless he *knows* and actually makes fewer mistakes.

The great general does not engage in formal reasoning on the battlefield. From his knowledge of history, from his experience, and from information received, suddenly comes the solution, and in Champagne Pétain repeats a maneuver of Wellington's. The great writer revises a sheet of manuscript by taking out a phrase or an adjective, or by changing the position of a verb. If we try to explain why these corrections improve the passage we shall undoubtedly succeed, but the writer had no need to do this. He has acquired the instinct for language by long and careful study of the styles of the masters. "The essential thing," says Valéry, "is not to find, but to integrate what we find." Knowledge is ours only if, at the moment of need, it offers itself to the mind without syllogisms or demonstrations for which there is no time.

For the great man of action the microcosm, or interior world, contains an exact replica of those parts of the outside world where his actions are to take place. A true statesman carries his country within him. He knows better than his cabinet members what the public's spontaneous reactions will be in a given situation. In order to acquire this perfect knowledge of his people, he had to reflect, observe, read, and become familiar with citizens of all classes. Now that he has mastered this knowledge, he expresses it in the form of decisions that are quick and just. The bureaucrat who has no feelers will consult newspapers, statistics, committees; and with all this information, oddly enough, he will make mistakes continually. Information is not culture. In the mind of a truly educated man, isolated facts are organized to make up a living world in the image of the real one. The statistician cuts up the world and kills it; the poet emulates a world and gives it life. The great man of action resembles the poet much more closely than he does the encyclopedist.

For the man of action, thought merges with action, just as for the poet it merges with image. We then understand the profound meaning of the following famous words: "Man is more capable than he knows;" "Belief must precede knowledge." Belief must precede knowledge because we must act before we know. The art of thinking is also the art of believing, because no human being at the present stage of civilization could safely call all his individual and social beliefs into question again or submit them to his conscience. To change all of one's opinions is a mental diversion which requires leisure for its indulgence. In order to live a life of action, man must accept most of the moral, social, and religious laws which have been recognized as necessary by his predecessors.

Our mind is made of superimposed layers, the first of which is formed by the beliefs of primitive humanity; the next by Asiatic, Greek, Roman, and Egyptian religions; the richest by Christianity; the thinnest by modern ideas regarding the structure of the universe. All of this constitutes our being; all of this is inscribed in our works of art, in our monuments, in our ceremonies, in our thoughts; *and a man cannot free himself from the past more easily than he can from his own body.* A solid thought is one whose foundations reach the deepest layers of instinct, even while its frontage and towers rise up into the clear luminous regions of the spirit. Thinking accepts the laws of logic which are its own laws. It observes, whenever it can, the rules of scientific research which have proved their virtues by their victories. It rests upon human traditions which survive in each one of us. It seeks and finds its most profound truths in art and religion. Finally, it thinks with the body and as such becomes action and poetry.

If I had to explain in a few words the relationship between theoretical thinking and applied thinking, I believe I would make use of the following comparison: in a battle, aircraft and infantry must collaborate. Aircraft go across the enemy lines, observe, clear, and formulate likely hypotheses regarding the trenches of the adversary. Aircraft must signal to infantry the directions in which advance seems possible, but aircraft cannot occupy the terrain. Of necessity, serious errors are often made in describing the terrain, which infantry will discover during its difficult advance. Infantry cannot fly over obstacles; it must destroy or surmount them and some of these will seem infinitely more dangerous at close sight than aircraft believed from their aerial observation. If infantry becomes entangled and blocked by the terrain, the role of aircraft will be, not to continue a useless advance, but to maintain contact with infantry, realize its errors of observation, and find out how to render assistance. Then the aircraft will set forth again on reconnaissance, and the constant collaboration between the executants on the ground and the observers in the sky may lead finally to victory.

It is thus that pure thinking can and must fly beyond the territory already colonized by convention and observation, over regions that are still hostile. Pure thinking describes what it believes it has seen after interpreting signs with hypotheses. Then comes action which, helped by the plans supplied by thinking, attempts to occupy these regions. Sometimes it succeeds; more often than not the action is rejected. Then, it is important that reason recognize its mistakes, regain contact with reality, and renouncing the idle notions condemned by experience suggest new hypotheses. It is only by means of the constant collaboration between reason, experience, and action that we can achieve—not a permanent victory, because such is not in the nature of things, but a moment of respite and repose underneath one of those fragile shelters which we call civilizations.

At the beginning we were asking ourselves: is it possible to draw in our spirit a true map of the universe, navigate according to this map towards definitive ends, and reach our chosen port? I believe our answer should be the following: human thinking cannot draw a precise map of the universe. It cannot set as goal the far and mythical shores of the kingdom of Utopia, but like the ancient navigators, it can bravely go from shipwreck to shipwreck, and from archipelago to archipelago, using the knowledge acquired by its ancestors, about the immutable constellations and about the capricious storms, completing this ancestral wisdom with actual experience, and observing the stars, the tides and the winds. This is sufficient, and the prudent Ulyses did not ask anything else from the gods.

II
THE ART OF LOVING

Art, Bacon said, is man added to nature. . . *"Ars est homo additus naturae."* Nature provides the raw elements of the paint, the sculpture, the poem, the drama. Man manages these elements and organizes them to satisfy the demands of his spirit. Once we admit this definition, which is excellent, it is evident that there exists an art of loving. Nature, in love as in anything else, only provides the crude elements: the division of the species into two sexes, the need to reproduce the species, and the powerful instincts placed at the service of these needs. But if the human mind had not modeled and composed these materials through the ages, our loves would not be much different from those between dogs. Observe in nature, in the air, in rivers the loves between animals; then read the *Princesse de Clèves* or the *Discours sur les Passions de l'Amour* and you will appreciate how widely separated, in love, are nature and art.

The miracle of human love is that, based on a very simple instinct, desire, it constructs buildings with the most complex and most delicate feelings. Because of love's magical operations, two humans form the most intimate communion. Because of love, two fragile, selfish, shy, inconsistent, and wild human beings, as we usually and naturally are, blend in the most delicious of relationships. In the eyes of two people, the indifference and hostility of the world, the uncertain future, the differences of class or nationality, suddenly vanish like smoke and frail dream. The power of desire permits them to conquer the barriers of selfishness and helps them accept others for what they really are. But desire is short-lived. How have men been able to evoke pure and lasting emotions from an instinct so capricious? This is this problem of the "sanctification of desire" that we must solve if we are to understand the art of loving. Before discussing this central point, it is first necessary to answer several preliminary questions.

1. — CHOOSING A PARTNER

Why, among the thousands of men and women we encounter, do we choose one rather than another upon whom to focus our thoughts? There are two theses which may be maintained, each containing a certain amount of truth.

The first one is that at certain periods of our life, particularly in adolescence, and then during the "mid-life crisis," *we are in the mood for love.* A vague desire, as yet impersonal, produces a pleasant sense of anticipation. At such moments a young man, lacking a real woman, gives himself up to the nymphs of his imagination; at such moments young girls fall in love with the heroes of novels, famous actors, or their literature professors. Youth is the most powerful of all love potions. "With this elixir," said Goethe, "you will see Helen in every woman." When the body anxiously awaits the arrival of the potential lover, the first agreeable person encountered may be the one to awaken love. Sometimes chance brings good fortune, and the encounter will produce a happy couple. Sometimes a man and a woman, joined together by an instant desire, will later discover differences and disagreements, and love will generate hatred.

We can also conceive *choices of a partner due to the circumstances of the encounter.* It often happens that shy people, who would not ordinarily admit their feelings and desires, find themselves brought into forced intimacies. Prisons during the Revolution brought out unsuspected amorous qualities in women who under more peaceful conditions would have been ordinary wives. In the eyes of women, a man's prestige, or his fame, envelops him in a luminous haze which obscures his faults. The moments of success are often suitable to the beginning of a love affair. Chance may also create the illusion of a mental or emotional affinity. Suddenly, on hearing a phrase uttered by a third person, two glances meet and reveal similar reactions. A car runs over a bump and two hands touch and remain in contact longer than necessary. That suffices.

The other thesis is that "the lightning flash," or love at first sight, *is the sign of predestination.* A Greek myth had it that human beings were originally composed of a man and a woman, that some god divided each being in two, and that these separated halves are continually searching for one another. When the two parts of a predestined couple meet, their rapport is announced to them by a violent and delicious impact, "the lightning flash." We all carry within "the original of *our* particular beauty whose copy we are searching for throughout the vast world," and if we find a real person possessing the charms with which we adorned nymphs figures of our adolescence, we abandon ourselves to the enchantment. There are people who both enchant our senses with their beauty and seduce our minds with the grace and charm of their conversation. We love them effortlessly and unreservedly. Every moment spent besides them makes us more certain of their perfection. We know that if we had been given the power to transform them, we would not wish to change anything; the sound of their voice is to us "the sweetest of harmonies" and their speech the most refined poem. To admire without reservation is a great joy; love which is founded upon mutual admiration of the mind as well as the body of the chosen person undoubtedly affords the most intense delights.

Finally, there is a rather large group of men and

women upon whom neither chance nor an irresistible impulse has imposed a life companion and who find themselves condemned to choose deliberately. Will an art of loving teach them a few general rules to guide them with their choice? It may be said that an even disposition, patience, and especially a good sense of humor, are virtues of great value in the happiness of a couple, and that all of them frequently, though not always, result from good health. The family of the chosen person must be carefully observed, because happiness begets happiness and love withers quickly in sad and constraint environments.

Women apparently achieve happiness more easily with energetic and virile men, and men achieve it easily with women who are affectionate and more easily willing to be led. Very young women say that they want to marry men whom they can dominate, but I have never discovered a woman who was truly happy with a man she did not admire for his strength and courage, nor a normal man who was perfectly happy with an Amazon. But all of this is quite complex, because even the most oppressed woman has a maternal instinct which finds satisfaction in seeing a child in her hero.

In fact, the role of chance is such that it is rare that a man and a woman truly choose a life companion by an act of pure volition, and it is better so: instinct, despite its mistakes, is more dependable here than intelligence. "The question 'Do I have to fall in love?' should not be asked; it must be felt within." The birth of love, like any birth, is the work of nature. It is later when the art of loving intervenes. We must now determine the exact moment at which the artist begins to model the rough materials.

2. — THE BIRTH OF LOVE

Stendhal has admirably described in his *De l'Amour* the birth of this emotion. Let us retain the essential points of his description and add to them what we have observed ourselves.

1.- In the origin of all love, there is an *impact*, produced either by admiration, or by some accident which reveals an understanding or arouses a desire. Absentmindedly, Wronsky steps off the train and says to himself: "Madame Karenina is very beautiful . . . What was the meaning of such a glance?" Charles Grandet comes into his cousin's life one afternoon in the romantic role of a sufferer. She would love him from that moment throughout her life.

2.- Once the impact has fixed our attention upon a person, absence is quite favorable to the birth of love. "The great strength of women," said Alain, "consists in being late or absent." It occurs that presence would soon reveal the weakness of him, or her, who has impressed us. During her absence, on the contrary, our beloved becomes one of the nymphs of our adolescence whom we can adorn with all of the attributes of perfection. Stendhal calls this process *crystallization.*

Because of this crystallization, the loved one is transformed into a different and superior person. That is why Proust said that love is subjective and that we do not love real people but only those whom we have created. This is no longer true in the case of legitimate admiration. There is no crystallization possible on a natural diamond. But there are very few diamonds without imperfections.

3.- When the first crystallization has been accomplished, a second encounter may take place without danger to love, because our emotion is such that *we will no longer be able to see the true person,* even if she is before us. We will replace her by the one created under crystallization. We will not hear the banal remarks, nor will we notice the lack of judgment and courage. The joy we experience is safe from interference because it is an inner joy.

4.- While things are in this state, love brings nothing but happiness, *but a fire cannot burn if it is not fed with fuel,* and the newborn flames will soon dwindle unless some breath of hope, however ephemeral, keeps them alight. As far as signs of encouragement are concerned, the lover is not hard to please. A glance, a pressure of hands, an enthusiastic reply, are immediately stimulating.

5.- If these signs are clear and continuous, a mutual love can be born and nothing is more beautiful, but it also happens that security and certainty kill the emotion. With many men and women, the beginnings of love are fed by doubts or, rather, by alternating coolness and encouragement. Frequently, this alternating of signs does not correspond to a real change in feelings. Shyness and chastity dictate the movements we would believe are inspired by disdain. We interpret as a sign, with the passion for detail possessed only by lovers and detectives, what was simply a headache, an ill-fitting belt, or a stocking with a run in it. A mere nothing is enough to worry a lover. He analyses looks, words, and gestures, finds hidden meanings, and tries to discover what faults he may have committed which can explain the rough treatment he is receiving. The less he understands (for there is nothing to understand), the more he thinks of the woman he loves and the deeper his love sinks into his mind. Love born of anxiety resembles a thorn shaped in such a way that efforts to pull it out of one's flesh merely cause it to penetrate more deeply therein.

6.- From this it seems that *flirting*, in other words

the deliberate game of alternatives, which consists in offering, withdrawing, and again offering the bait, seems to be made to awaken and sustain love. As a kitten leaps upon the ball of wool that is held out and then drawn back, so our young human prey allows himself to be trapped by the games of a flirtatious woman. Pursuing what is withheld and refusing what is offered are natural impulses and they are easily explained.

7.- *But prolonged flirting destroys love.* Madame Récamier, a famous and for a long time invincible coquette, took it into her head to make Benjamin Constant fall in love with her, and indeed she succeeded. "Try," she said to him, and the hope of success immediately made a child of this mature man. He thought, "She doesn't love me, but she likes me." When he discovered the game, he suffered: "I've never known a coquette. What a pest!" A little later: "God, how I hate her." Then came a decrystallization: "I give it up. She's caused me a terrible day. She has the brain of a bird and neither memory, judgment, nor taste." Thus, a coquette may go too far. Célimène, in the fifth act of *Le Misanthrope,* is abandoned by all those who had at first been charmed by her wit and her beauty.

8.- If, in the manner of a doctor who alternatively introduces poisonous gas and oxygen into the lungs of a person on the operating table, the coquette blends the disdain with sufficient hope to keep her patient alive, this cruel game is almost irresistible. Must this game be played? I believe that *the best of men and women are willing to renounce, either because of love or kindness of heart, the almost certain advantages to be gained by flirting.* There is some greatness when saying: "I know that in declaring my love I put myself in your power, but it pleases me to do so." If the partner is unworthy of this confidence, it is necessary to occasionally administer homeopathic dosages of flirting. If the partner is worthy of this total openness, a beautiful love shared and mutually trusting can exist.

9.- The early stages of *mutual love* are rightly considered to be the more delightful: a double crystallization has occurred and it resists presence. We rise above ourselves to become what the other wanted us to be. When such a state as this lasts, the result is a beautiful existence for two people.

It is rare, even in love like this, for two emotions to be equal in strength, and if they are, that they last. Most of us have to conquer and ceaselessly reconquer the person we desire, who is not offered to us without a struggle.

3. — ATTRACTING LOVE

Is it possible to make someone love us? And, first

of all, is it necessary? If love does not correspond to love, is it not easier to insist upon the enjoyment of pleasure? Such was the case in primitive or archaic civilizations. If a man desired a woman, he abducted her, and thus a couple was formed. The captive was at the mercy of the warrior. It often happened that she came to love him because he had chosen her, he was her master, or simply because he was kind. In later times *wealth* and *power* played the role *physical strength* had. Wealth is not as easily loved as courage, because wealth is not a quality of the lover himself. In spite of that, Jupiter reached even Danae disguised as a shower of gold.

However, the love of slaves does not bring happiness to demanding souls. *We want to be chosen, not endured.* Conquest brings no lasting happiness unless the person conquered was possessed of free will. Only then can there be doubt and anxiety and those continual victories over habit and boredom which are the source of the sweetest emotions. The beauties of the harem are rarely loved, for they are prisoners.

Inversely, the beauties of the American beaches do not inspire love, because they are completely liberated. Where is love's victory when there is neither veil, modesty, nor moral to oppose its advances? Excessive freedom raises the transparent walls of an invisible harem around the crowd of easy women. *Romantic love*

requires that women, without being inaccessible, live a life
within the rather narrow limits of religion and convention.
These conditions, admirably observed in the Middle
Ages, originated the courtly love.   Then the woman
remained in the castle, a landlady surrounded by honor;
the knight departed for the Crusades and through the
trails of the world thought about his lady.   Marching
with the horses, crystallization was accomplished easily,
while back in the country, the ever present and distant
castilian lady awakened in the page who had remained
near her, emotions which will later be deformed by the
Revolution, those of Julien Sorel for Madame de Rênal.
The preceptor is along the lines of the page; in between
is Chérubin, a page now uninhibited and unafraid.

During the times of the courtly love, the lover scarcely
ever tried to arouse love in the object of his passion. He
resigned himself to loving in silence, or at least without
hope.   This was even the case with Monsieur de
Numours and Princess de Clèves.   Some judge these
passions as naive and unreal, *but to certain sensitive*
souls this kind of remote admiration is extremely
pleasurable, and those who are absolutely subjective are
better protected against deception and disillusion. "The
pleasure of love without daring to declare it has its
thorns, but also its sweetness. Is it not a joy to organize
all of our actions in order to please a person whom we
infinitely admire? Every day we study to find the means
to discover ourselves and we spend the time as if we

were speaking with the person we love. The eyes brighten up and dwindle in an instant; and even though it is not seen that the woman who causes all of this traumatism keeps a distance, there is at least the satisfaction of feeling all of these movements for a person who truly deserves them."

If an adolescent falls in love with an actress whom he has seen only on the stage, he adorns her with the spiritual perfections which her voice and her face seem to indicate that she possesses but which she undoubtedly does not. He has met her in a play as a character dreamed by Marivaux or Musset and imagines her to be as poetically charming as the heroine she impersonates. Because he has only contemplated her under the flattering glow of the stage lights, he is unaware of her age and the wrinkles upon her face. Because he has never shared his life with her, he knows nothing of her bad temper or her vanity. Byron said "It is easier to die for the woman one loves than to live with her." The girl who admires a novelist will generously grant him the grace of his heroes; she does not suspect his rheumatic joints, his painful indigestion, his lethargic character, or his irritability. *It is easy to be admired when one remains inaccessible.*

In order to save love, is it then necessary not to try to inspire it, or to remain unknown? No, because those intellectual loves, as beautiful as they are in the beginning, cannot last. "The longer the road to love, the deeper is the pleasure experienced by the sensitive soul." Yes, but nevertheless the road must, after much delightful winding, lead to its end without losing itself in the wilderness. Otherwise, love would end by falling asleep and dying of starvation. "Without the help of its fountain its glory will diminish." Sooner or later the lover feels an imperative desire to be loved.

Then, what can the art of loving teach? Recipes of love potions, magic spells? Ancient poetry and fairy tales are full of enchantresses, and we know that today, as in the times of Theocritus or Ovid, in countless of sordid backrooms in Paris, London and New York, the age-old anguished question is asked a hundred times a day to some horrible crone: "What can I do to make him love me?" To this cry, the equally-long experience of humanity replies, as it does with all cries, with rituals and ceremonies.

4. — COURTSHIP

The set of ceremonies, maneuvers, and games by which lovers strive to attract each other is called *courtship*. Animals, like human beings, do their courting during mating seasons. Let us indicate the usual methods of seduction, from the crudest, which are common to all species, to the noblest, which are used by man.

a) *Adornment.-* The purpose of adornment is to attract the attention to he or she who wears it. Flowers, by the splendor of their color, attract insects to bring them the necessary pollen at the right moment; fireflies and glow worms illuminate themselves at night in order to make their kind know that they are available for love; similarly women, by the grace or boldness of their gowns, offer themselves to the election of men. A young woman has both the right and duty to be attractive. All of them, or nearly all, make efforts to this end. Imprudent virgins rely upon the immodesty of their dresses; wise ones upon the more lasting allurement of mystery. Most of them follow the fashion, the sole object of which is to attract the attention of the opposite sex. Apparel makers, fashion designers, and jewelers make a living of this constant desire to surprise.

Some women, either from affectation or disdain, disregard the laws of fashion, but in a society where all women, from the worker to the duchess, comply simultaneously with similar forms, the greatest originality is to refuse uniformity. Thus, the simplest becomes the least simple; the least flirtatious the most flirtatious of all; the lack of adornment becomes an adornment itself. During pre-Raphaelite days, the young English women who went to William Morris's house on Sundays wore plain dresses of blue serge and yellow amber necklaces, but they were very noticeable among the other women who remained faithful to the elaborate jewelry and dress ornamentation of the late Victorian period.   The artist attracts attention with his wide-brimmed hat, the young writer with his leather jacket, and the *dandy* of earlier days with his velvet waistcoats. In many animal species, it is the male who turns to adornment.   The peacock is one of nature's triumphs over art.   In the human species, where the male has a certain tendency to avoid the economic responsibilities of the union, the woman must spend more care upon her adornment.   This is true, at least in France.

b) *Virtuosity.-* To do whatever it may be, anything at all, better than other people is another method of pleasing. Every lover strives to show his virtuosity, and the ways of doing it are infinite. Certain birds dive into the water in front of the partner and extract from the bottom of the lake some aquatic herbs which they offer to the mate. When asked "What will you be searching for in the Orient?" Chateaubriand replied: "Fame, so that I will be loved," and from this plunge into the Mediterranean Sea he brought back some immortal phrases for Madame de Noailles.   Novels have been written, such as Sainte-Beuve's *Le Clou d'Or*, for women who must have found therein emotions depicted especially to move them. Almost all composers have transformed their laments and their desires into harmonious pieces. However, a tennis player is also attractive merely by the perfection of his backhand strokes, the driver by his daring, and the ballerina by the agility of her toes.

The reputation of a womanizer gives a man the most dangerous power. Wise virgins resist him, but foolish virgins frequently yield to the desire to take a celebrated lover from a rival, even from a friend. This is a complex emotion, made up of vanity, respect for another woman's taste, and the need to establish self-confidence by winning a difficult victory. Don Juan chose his first lovers; later on, he was chosen. Byron said "Since the Trojan War no one has been as abducted as me."

The need of security, very marked in women, draws the weaker among them to men who, by their strength or power, seem to offer them a solid support. In time of war they count a warrior's medals; in time of peace they hunt for genius or wealth. To the man in love the giving of presents is a way of asserting his power. The penguin and the banker offer pebbles of varying brilliance to their respective loved ones. The finch presents twigs and leaves to its mate as the young man presents woolen threads in the form of rugs and tapestry to his fiancé. The swallow and the woman think about the nest from the moment they have chosen their males.

c) *Praise*.- Praise is a way of offering or gift. Almost all love poems consist of praise or lament. The lament may produce emotion, but soon becomes tiresome. Praise is pleasing because almost all men and women, even the most arrogant, have some sort of *inferiority complex*. The loveliest woman distrusts her intelligence; the strongest man distrusts his charm. It is delightful to reveal to someone a thousand qualities, which make him lovable, and which he ignored or neglected. Certain shy and melancholic women blossom like flowers in the sun when they are admired. As for men, there is no limit to their appetite for praise. Many plain and unattractive women have been loved all their lives because they knew how to praise. Note: people are pleased when praised, not for their obvious qualities with which they are familiar, but for those which they believe they lack. A general will not thank you for talking to him about his victories, but he will be eternally grateful if you mention his flashing eyes. The famous novelist cares little for praise of his novels, but if you speak enthusiastically about some obscure essay, which was one of his failures, or about the vibrant quality of his voice, he will immediately become interested.

d) *Female Courtship*.- Women have their own particular methods of conquest. For a long time she has imposed the following fiction: that she awaits the advances of men. This is based merely upon appearances. Shaw says "A woman will wait for a man, but as the spider does for the fly." Today Amazons, quite numerous indeed, fight with the breast uncovered. The object of dancing has always been to overcome man's shyness and at the same time to compel him to control his desires. Modern dancing has a far more sensual purpose than the ancient or village variety. It remains one of the most effective stratagems in the species.

One of the essential roles of women in the urban civilization, and one which really helps them to be loved, is to be intermediaries between man and nature. Many men trapped in sedentary jobs have lost all contact with the universe. The woman who would pull a man out of his monotonous existence and returns to him the joy of the woods, lakes, mountains and the ocean, is endowed with all the beauty she reveals to him.

"Men were made for battle; women for the rest of the warrior." The art of loving is often, for women, the art of providing diversion, encouragement, and moral support. Consider Madame de Maintenon's conquest of Louis XIV. Never did an undertaking seem so hopeless. Madame de Maintenon was no longer young; her only connection with the king was that of governess for the children he had by Madame de Montespan, a very beautiful woman who exercised a powerful influence upon his mind. Madame de Maintenon not only took Louis XIV from her dazzling rival, but she also succeeded in accomplishing what Madame de Montespan had not even dared to hope for: she persuaded the king to marry her.

What was the secret of her success? First of all, she approached the king as a messenger of peace when the king began to be tired of the scenes of his lover. Men can endure for a while the explosions of anger and jealousy of a loved woman. Some like the agitation in love as the storm in the ocean. But the majority of them are peaceful. *Good* sense of humor, simplicity, and kindness easily conquers them, especially if some mad woman has previously cured them from their taste for violence.

The second secret of Madame de Maintenon: every night she attended the work sessions of the king, who summoned his ministers in her house. She listened to the reports in silence, but if the king asked her, she replied with and intelligent reflection that showed she had been attentive, understanding, and judging. This was a skillful attitude, *because every man worthy of the name cares about his work more than anything in the world, even more than the woman he loves.* Does such a woman try to distract him from his job to make herself the center of his life? He may initially let her do it, not without resentment, but the time will come when he will belong to the woman who would place his work at the forefront.

e) *Culture.*- Birds sing their songs and plunge into action by themselves. Crabs perform by themselves their love acrobatics in the ponds. But men have invented prestige and virtuosity by proxy. Instead of composing his own poem, the lover reads Baudelaire's to his lover. To be loved, the pianist plays a piece by Chopin. The genius of the master is reflected upon his interpreters and admirers. The emotions that he incites, by being attached to a presence, enrich an image and beautify it with memories. By imposing a beautiful order and a super-human joy, music frequently predisposes its souls to love. Beethoven, Mozart, and Wagner have brought more than a couple together. Many relationships start at the museum. The reading of beautiful novels together brings conversation topics and models of conduct to the lovers. The best novels are lessons in love that show how the passions should be lived by those who deserve them. *Sharing similar cultural interests permits to maintain a high level of imagination and enthusiasm.* This lets us pass through difficult times when satiety "leaves a bitter taste in the midst of the pleasures." To devote time to culture is to prepare to love.

f) *A Common Faith.*- Wether it is a religious faith, national or political faith, or faith in the necessity and beauty of a lifework, if shared, is a marvelous strengthening of love. It is indeed difficult for a passionate believer to experience a permanent emotion for the person who does not in any way share his beliefs.

If "love is the joy accompanied by the idea of an external cause," such love will be necessarily upset by a painful disagreement. Then love can only be saved by an infinite tact and respect on the part of the unbeliever, or a hope for a conversion on the part of the believer, which will be frequently brought by love. *One may be assured of happiness by sharing without reserve the faith of the man or woman one loves.* In this way, our intellectual as well as our emotional force propels us in the chosen direction. All work done with love is a delight, but nothing in the world can equal the joy of a true mingling of work and love. This perfect mingling sometimes produces those wonderful pairs of scholars, artists, apostles, who are both couples and teams. Here courtship is useless; it has been replaced by a "communion."

5. — AVOIDING MONOTONY

After a long or short courtship, subtle or naive, love comes into being, but infant mortality is high in the city of love. In order to nurture love, constant care is necessary. Novelty, the most potent of all attractions, is also the most perishable. At the beginning of a love relationship, each has a thousand discoveries to make in the other. Everyone shares youthful memories, pictures, songs, anecdotes which, mingled with caresses, fill with delight the first days of leisure. But these reserves soon dwindle and the stories which seemed so new are now boring, timeworn. How many men and women become brilliant when separated from their habitual companions because they can talk without embarrassment about things already discussed too often. Observe the couples sitting in tables at restaurants. The duration of silence between couples is too often proportional to the length of their life together.

This is the case of couples without inventiveness, for inventiveness in love consists in bringing a continuous novelty to a relationship. He who truly loves finds a perpetual delight in wanderings every day among the thoughts of his beloved, just as a village priest finds joy in strolling the narrow paths of his small garden every afternoon.

Some are always faithful, either because they learned to regard love as a serious matter or because they are shy and home loving. Certain happy relationships are founded upon a mutual distaste for the conflicts of the outside world, upon a wish to live a secluded domestic life among familiar people and things, upon the desire for security, etc. But he who loves with more intensity than this learns, if necessary, how *to renew* himself. "Everyday one exhausts all means of pleasing; and nevertheless one must please and one does please." This may not even require a conscious effort. If a person has charm, he always has it, and charm never fatigues. Every word, every act, of a person with charm is a constant delight. Old age does not change one in this respect. A beautiful face ages gracefully and it is a joy to find beneath white hair the look and the smile that one once loved beneath dark or blond hair.

Is there an art of not tiring people? The great secret is to act naturally. An unnatural attitude is difficult to maintain and it always lacks beauty. Thus, wise lovers strive to preserve their companions' natural dispositions. There are men who attempt to mold women, imposing their tastes and ideas on them. This is sheer madness! If a woman is too different from our ideal, let us not love her, but if we have freely chosen her, let us allow her to be herself. In friendship, as in love, we are happy to see only those with whom it is possible to be ourselves without embarrassment or pretense.

Skillful lovers are also careful to arrange encounters in naturally beautiful places. Out of this has grown the very judicious custom of the honeymoon, but it is not necessary to travel that far. A loving woman instinctively knows how to arrange her own decor. Some display adorable skill to bring the enchantments of nature and art. They predict when their lovers desire secluded companionship and when they feel the need of a concert or a stroll. It is the woman who is always more deeply aware of the social aspects of life than the man and in her hands should be left the management of romances.

On the other hand, if a man does not want to exhaust such good will and such touching affection, he must understand the *importance of the part played by love in the life of a woman.* Nothing is more stupid than the man who, from the heights of a philosophy or a doctrine, is contemptuous of a woman's ideas. They differ from his, but they are more concrete, simpler, and wiser. If he is at odds with his lover, he will never be able to persuade her by means of argument but by means of affection, silence, and patience. He must not forget that she is far more subject to her emotions during a large part of her existence than he. If during these difficult moments, a man attributes a bad temper, to what is merely the complaint of an ailing body, he risks, for nothing more than a passing state, the destruction of what has been and may continue to be a happy union. It is a trivial but a fair image to compare the impulses of a woman's soul to the movements of the ocean. The wise husband never becomes exasperated. Like the mariner in a storm, he slackens sail, waits attentively, and the storm does not prevent him from loving the sea.

Some rules in the art of not tiring the loved one should be common to both sexes. *The first is to show in the most intimate moments as much politeness as that during the first encounter.* For well-born people, courtesy is not incompatible with being natural. All things may be said graciously and it would be a strange confusion to imagine brutality as the only satisfactory expression of frankness. *The second rule is to maintain in all circumstances a sense of humor that allows to laugh at one self,* to recognize the ridiculousness of most disagreements, and *not to attach a tragic importance to the collection of grievances that occur in every conjugal life.* It is useless to aggravate each argument with memories of past quarrels. *The third rule is to maintain jealousy within reasonable limits,* that is to avoid indifference and distrust which are both hurtful. *The fourth is to allow a fresh crystallization by means of an occasional separation;* amorous or conjugal vacations may be dangerous, but if they are short and broken by letters they can play a useful role. Two people will sometimes, through familiarity and indolence, lose the note of tenderness in their conversations and this can be recovered by means of the written phrase. Finally, *the last rule,* and the most secret, is to *continue the romance:* "Why, when I have won her, do I continue to court her? Because, though she belongs to me, she is not and never will be mine. . ." An excellent point to consider for the women who deserve it.

But "not wearying" one's beloved would be a rather futile art to practice, if in spite of it all one wearied of her. Is there also an art of not becoming tired? Or must it be admitted that there are two species of men and women: the faithful and the unfaithful, the steady and the unsteady, and that if one belongs to one group, it is quite useless to pretend to be from the other? I believe that in this as in all things nature provides certain materials which must be regulated by the will. A man or a woman is not born unsteady; he or she becomes one after the early amorous experiences. They may be passionate by temperament and encounter partners who are frigid. When this happens, if they are moral they will be faithful and unhappy. If they are amoral, they will be unfaithful and restless until they meet their complementary "halves" and are suddenly transformed. There are people who have lived an adventurous existence which abruptly comes to an end with the discovery of the proper companion.

So much for physical instability, but there is also psychic instability. Don Juan is not always a man of an exacting character; the female "Don Juan" is often an indifferent woman. Her conquests thus provide her with pleasures of pride and imagination. The pride of the man or the woman diminishes when they experience lack of self-confidence. Byron heard the first young woman he fell in love with say: "How can I interest myself in this cripple?" And he spent the rest of his life avenging himself. A woman will aggressively break any relationship with which she is acquainted because, as a girl, she was thought to be ugly. Feeling the need of self assurance, she will continuously find proof of her power. An insatiable imagination frequently results from a romantic, that is to say, an unreal childhood. Chateaubriand went from one woman to another, because, in his youth, he was tormented by desire and deprived of women who could satisfy it; he created an image of the ideal woman, the Nymph, for whom he searched all his life. Mistress after mistress disappointed him until the day when age made him more indulgent and he believed he had discovered the embodiment of the Nymph: Juliette Récamier.

Against this psychic instability, the priest and the doctor may sometimes work with success, because when the sufferer begins to understand the nature of the problem, he finds himself liberated. If it is incurable, he should at least try to do as little harm as possible, and to carefully avoid taking faithful individuals as objects of his temporary loves. Informal love for the fun of it may be forgiven, but it is a real crime to awaken a lasting passion in someone just for the fun of it.

6. — THE SANCTIFICATION OF DESIRE

True sanctity consists in humility, sweetness, and charity, rather than in religious ecstasies and mortifications. Similarly, true love may be recognized, not by the violent assaults of passionate desire, but by the perfect and lasting harmony of daily life. Reverend Huvelin relates a story of a young nun who once asked Saint Teresa to teach her what holiness was. She expected to be told about visions, but the saint simply took her to a convent she had just founded, where the nun encountered nothing but inconvenience, difficulty, disappointment, defeat, complaints, and work, for several months. At last, the young nun dared to ask when she was to be shown what holiness was. "Holiness?" said Saint Teresa of Ávila. "It is nothing more than to endure each day with patience and love the life we have lived in this convent."

The glorious feasts of passion which are known to joyful lovers resemble those summer days when the warmth of the sun fills us with blissful dreaminess; when the purity of the sky is so clear that we cannot imagine it tarnished by clouds; and when the humblest village of the plain, transfigured by light, becomes a fairy-tale miracle. The enchanted memories left by such beautiful days, and the hope to relive similar ones, provide us with the necessary strength and courage to endure dark stormy months. But because neither summer nor desire can outlast its natural term we must learn to love gray days, autumn mists, and long winter evenings. "The most beautiful love feelings," says Abel Bonnard, "must resemble a rich festal robe made of flowered silk and lined with another which has no design but it is of such a rare and delicate shade that one almost prefers it to the flowered silk."

What is this soberer and gentler happiness which comes in the early moments of love to take its place by the side of desire, at first shyly but soon with a sweet authority? Of what is this love made which is born of desire and outlives it? Of confidence, habit, and admiration. Almost all human beings disappoint us, but a few of us have known the joy of meeting a woman or a man whose sincerity and frankness have never disappointed us, who in almost every situation has behaved as we wished, and who in our most difficult moments has not abandoned us. Those few are familiar with that marvelous feeling: confidence. With at least one person, for a little while each day, they are able to lift the heavy visor of their armored helmets, breathe freely, and show their faces and their hearts without fear.

Confidence is such a precious thing that, like physical desire, it lends charm to the most insignificant acts. In their young days a man and a woman sought moments of solitude to hug each other; now they seek them in order to confide in one another. The times for a stroll together have become as important to them as the times of their former dates. They both feel themselves to be perfectly understood and nurtured; they think the same things at the same time; each one suffers physically when the other is in mental distress; each would give his or her life for the other and the other knows it. No doubt a perfect friendship can also inspire such emotions, but friendships without reservations are infinitely rare while a great love can endow the simplest person with discernment, abnegation, and self confidence.

How shall the life of a happy couple in the autumn of their love be described? How can it be shown that the god is still a god, though he may have acquired a mortal face? It is not easy. The symphony of happiness, orchestrated by a composer of genius, can be sublime; a mediocre musician can do better with stormy themes. The ascending notes of the prelude to *Parsifal,* which are gradually higher and purer, lift the listener's soul above the music itself; the *Béatitudes* of Franck, and *the Requiem* of Fauré evoke better than words what could be a wonderful renaissance, the natural and powerful crescendo of an indestructible harmony. And if I have cited a Requiem mass is because the idea of death is the only dissonance in these too perfect love relations.

An admirable poem by Coventry Patmore expresses the despair of a man who, after a long life of happiness, is suddenly confronted by the dead body of the woman who was the whole world to him. Painfully, sorrowfully, and tenderly he reproaches her for having abandoned him:

"This is so much unlike your noble and gracious ways ...
Don't you ever repent, oh love of my life,
Of that July afternoon, without a kiss, or a good-bye,
With a frightened glance, and an unintelligible phrase,
Departed for such a long journey? ...
Indeed, it was unlike your noble and gracious ways."

It is both the danger and the nobility of love to risk everything upon the existence of one person, and such a fragile one.

But against the greatest of loves death itself is powerless. Once in Spain, I came across an old peasant woman of extraordinary dignity, who said to me: "Oh, I have no reason to complain... Of course I have suffered in my life, but when I was twenty I fell in love with a young man . . . He loved me and we were married . . . He died in a few weeks, but in any case I had my share of happiness, and for fifty years I have lived on his memory." It is a powerful consolation to be able to evoke at least one perfect memory during the times of sorrow and loneliness. For a shadeless love, for the luminous and sweet images with which love fills our thoughts, like the works of great artists, like the deep religious faith, man participates in something above himself. Out of the sudden impact of his instincts, he has drawn a divine spark.

How? I believe it was futile to attempt to describe

it. "Love does not need analysts, but poets." The last word about the art of loving does not come from Stendhal but from Mozart, as Stendhal himself has frequently stated. Go to a concert; listen to the pure and enchanting musical tones, and if your love then seems confusing, sour, and discordant, it is because you have yet to learn the art of loving. But if you recognize this perfection in your own feelings, this same wonderful understanding, this same sublime reconciliation of the themes above any dissonance, then you shall experience one of the rarest adventures worth living, a great love.

III
THE ART OF WORKING

"The joy of the soul is in the action."
Shelley

In the end, what is the exact meaning of the verb "to work"? Let us consult Littré's dictionary: *"TO WORK: To take pains in the accomplishment of a task."* This does not seem to us like a very good definition. Why "to take pains"? Can one not take pleasure in work? Let us close the dictionary and consider some examples. A glass blower works. What does he make? He is given a formless mass which he shapes into a useful article. What does the miner do? He removes raw materials from the earth, such as coal and iron, and gives them to men who will transform them into power, heat, and tools. What does the farmer do? He plows the earth, prepares it, and sows it with seed at the appropriate spot. What does the novelist do? He puts into narrative form the material resulting from his observations of humans and transforms this shapeless mass into a work of art, just like the glass blower. What does the student do? He tries to make a part of himself the knowledge acquired by humanity before him; he puts his mind in order; he makes *himself.* To work is to impose on things and creatures of nature transformations or movements that will render them more useful or more beautiful; it is also to study the laws governing these transformations, formulate them, or apply them.

1. — RECIPES OF WORK

Although man's labors are innumerable and varied, there should be a few maxims common to all workers.

a) *One must choose among the possible vocations.* A man's power and intelligence have narrow limits. He who wants to do everything will never do anything. We know very well those people of uncertain abilities who say: "I could be a great musician," or "Business would be easy for me," or "If a worked in politics I would surely be a success." We may be certain that they will always be amateur musicians, bankrupt businessmen, and failed politicians. Napoleon held that the art of war consisted of making oneself strongest at a certain point; the art of living consists in choosing a point of attack and concentrating on it our forces. The choice of a career must not be left to chance. The beginner must aks himself "What sort of job am I fitted for? What are my natural abilities?" It is useless to ask from someone what he cannot provide. If you have a fearless son, make him an airplane pilot rather than the head of an office. But once the choice is made, let there be no regrets unless a serious accident occurs.

Within the chosen career new choices will then be necessary. A writer cannot write *every* sort of novel; a statesman cannot reform *every* administration; a traveler cannot visit *every* country. Here again, one must discard without regret temptations to undertake projects beyond our control. Grant yourself the time required to make your choice, but not an unlimited time. Having carefully considered the consequences of a command, army officers usually put an end to the debate with the word "Execution!" Thus, put an end to your own interior debates. "What am I going to do next year? Shall I study for this examination, or that one? Travel abroad? Start working in this factory?" It is natural that these questions be carefully debated at length, but it is also necessary to set a deadline after which a decision must be made. Once made, "Execution!" Afterwards regrets would be sterile and changes would be futile.

In order to guarantee adherence to the choice made, it is a good idea to write down, from time to time, a work plan indicating both immediate and long-term objectives. When referring to this plan, after several months or several years, we become aware of our abilities and our limitations. Within the elements of the plan, it is necessary to identify the one that requires immediate action. All attention should be focused on this element. Do what you do, *age quod agis*, put your whole heart into it. Strive with both your body and your mind towards the goal. When it has been reached, you may retrace your steps, explore the path which cut across your own, look into a nearby scenario. But until the work is done, no exploring of alternatives.

Amicable men are those who are interested in everything; men who accomplish things, who finish their tasks, are those who, during a given period of time interest themselves in one thing only. In America , these men are said to possess "single-track minds;" their tenacity and their obsession are sometimes fastidious; their repeated attacks end with demolishing all obstacles to success.

b) *One must believe in the possibility of success*: If an objective has been well chosen, it means it has been selected such that your aptitudes will enable you, barring accidents, to achieve it. It is useless and dangerous to undertake an unattainable objective. Failure risks the destruction of self-confidence and effort. Goethe advised young poets to write short poems rather than an epic. Samuel Butler said "We must always eat the best grapes in the bunch first." It is healthy to write the easier portions of a long and complex book first. If a journey is too long to accomplish in one stretch, there is nothing more legitimate than dividing it into stages and devoting full attention to each one, just like the mountaineer looks at each step he cuts in the ice and refuses to turn his eyes up towards the summit, which would frighten him, nor down into the depths, which would terrify him.

To write the history of a country seems at first a superhuman undertaking. Divide it into periods. Apply yourself to the one you know best, then to the one that follows. One day you will be surprised to find that you have reached the end of your efforts, and you will look with astonishment upon the high wall of ice that you have climbed. After a few experiments, the heart takes courage and our breath becomes more steady. An author who has written a great many books no longer has any doubts at his ability to finish the one he is beginning. He dares, like Martin du Gard, Duhamel, or Jules Romains, to attempt the ascent of a huge pile of books. He is certain of one day reaching its summit.

When a Lyautey arrives in Morocco, he finds a country in dissolution, without leaders, without finance, without an army. Another would have despaired at the task of putting an order to that. But he applies himself to consolidating his power over the cities he holds: Rabat and Fez. Starting from these centers, he radiates from tribe to tribe, diffuses his politics like an oil plume, makes slow and gradual gains, and after a long effort reduces dissidence to a thin fringe. In a similar manner, "the farmer cutting hay does not look towards the far end of the field." In a similar manner, the dedicated lady who wants a thorough cleaning attacks her cupboards shelf by shelf. The fool thinks everything is easy and comes in for many disappointments; the coward believes all is impossible and gives up before beginning; the good worker knows that great things are possible, and prudently, little by little, he accomplishes them.

c) *One must have a work discipline.* Many complain that life is short, but are these people even alive for eight hours a day? The amount of work that can be accomplished by a man who is at his working desk at dawn every day, or at his bench, or in his shop, is astounding. Consider the fact that a writer who produced only two pages a day would have at the end of a long life, equaled in quantity, though certainly not in quality, the writings of Balzac or Voltaire.

But it is not enough to sit at a desk; one must be protected. The effectiveness of work increases in geometrical proportion if there are no interruptions. This is evident for the writer who needs a training time to forget about the outside world and concentrate only upon his own ideas and images; this is also true for the mechanic who is searching for the cause of a breakdown, or for the manufacturing manager who is occupied with getting out his orders. Discontinued work always shows the traces of interruptions.

Thus, it is the duty of the worker to keep clear of

time-wasters or, as Montherlant calls them, chronophages. The *importunes* of Molière. They are pitiless. From the man who does not resist them, they will take the last moment of his time without considering that if left alone he might do valuable work. They are unscrupulous. The hardened chronophage will go to the chief of the army general staff the day a war is declared to describe the military situation according to his janitor. Chronophages function by visit, by telephone, and by mail. Kindness and patience with them are grave faults. They must be treated ruthlessly, since accepting them would be suicide.

Goethe is a master in this regard when he said: "It is absolutely necessary to break the people's habit of dropping by unannounced. They want us to be interested in their affairs. Their visits would only fill our minds with ideas different from our own, which we do not need. I have enough with my own ideas, which I never seem to carry to their proper conclusion." And then again: "He who wishes to do something for the world must not let himself be taken by it." A most legitimate defense since it would be the world the first to blame him in case of failure for giving in too easily. "It is not good that you go out so much," say the chronophages, "you are neglecting your work." Then they add: "Come for dinner tomorrow." We must learn the lesson and decline the invitation.

When, despite the orders given, an importune forced his way into Goethe's house, he was quickly discouraged by the great man's glacial attitude. Goethe put both hands behind his back and remained quiet. If his visitor was someone of importance, Goethe cleared his throat and uttered a few "Hum, hum, so. . . so. . .," which soon brought the conversation to an end. With his letters he divided them into two classes: those asking for something (these were thrown in the garbage); and those offering something; and only if the latter contained proposals of some advantage to him would he answer them. Even then he said: "Oh, young people, you do not yet know the value of time!"[2]

It may be said that such egoism is cruel, that there are some very famous men who do reply to letters, and that, among importunes, there are to be found some individuals worthy of attention, sympathy, and even affection. Many people complained about Goethe and found certain inhuman quality in him, but it was this inhuman quality that enabled him to leave us with *Faust* and *Wilhelm Meister.* In fact, he who allows himself to be devoured will be devoured, and he will die before he has done his work. The man who has an untamed passion for his work asks of others *only that which can support this work.* He does not avoid any useful work that he can do well, but he flies from conversations, meetings,

---

[2] Robert d'Harcourt, *Goethe et l'art de vivre.*

talks, and gossip chats, which leave behind only phrases. Goethe even advises such a man to ignore daily events if he cannot do anything about them. If we spend an hour every morning informing ourselves about distant wars and another hour lamenting their possible consequences, when we are neither ministers, generals, nor journalists, nor anything, we render no service to our country and we waste the most irrecoverable of our possessions: our own short and unique life.

d) In the case of Goethe, this discipline in work extended to a *discipline in emotion*. It is true that if we abandon ourselves unreservedly to our emotional impulses, we often render ourselves incapable of doing any work. These impulses are natural and one cannot advise men to sacrifice their emotional lives in all circumstances to their work. But two rules must be remembered and observed: the first is *not to allow ourselves to be turned away from our work by empty or exaggerated emotions* (how many lost college degrees can be accounted for by the whims of a coquette!) ; the second is *to sacrifice everything to certain works which justify such a sacrifice*. This was the case of Proust who gave his life to finish his novel; this is also the case of a national leader in wartime or in some serious crisis. Joffre repressed his emotions, and some of his friends complained about his ruthlessness, but this ruthlessness made possible the reestablishment on the Marne.

e) *Great workers are always, or almost always, men who know how to go into seclusion from time to time.* They have their country *village*, mountain cabins, isolated beaches where they shed all responsibility, even toward people to whom they are bound by affection and friendship. Only there do events and emotions take their proper place in the great scheme of things. In the tumult of a large city, a scene, an article, or a commentary, seem to have some importance; they take the place of serious work and of true feelings; beneath the slow turning of the stars, insignificant things recede into the shades and become invisible. Then, in the silence of the night and of the soul, the foundations of lasting edifices are erected upon grounds cleared of rubbish and futility. "Oh, solitude," said Barrès, "you alone have not degraded me!" Oh, solitude, it must be added, you alone have not debilitated me!

2. — ADMINISTRATORS, LIEUTENANTS, ASSISTANTS

Until now, we have studied the case of the worker who chooses his own work, is free to do it or abandon it, and must impose his own discipline because no one else will do so. We must now mention those who are not themselves creators or leaders, but whose mission it is to assist such persons. In this category are aides, chiefs of staff, departmental heads, assistants. These professions have their own set of rules. Those who practice them are not required to develop the general plans of action, but to make their creation and execution easier for those who employ them. This requires special qualities.

a) *Modesty*. A man who works as part of a team under orders from a boss must be without vanity. If he has too strong a will of his own and if his ideas are in conflict with those of his boss, the execution of orders will lack security because of his efforts to interpret them in his own direction. Faith in the chief is the link that will keep the team together.

Naturally, deference must not turn into servility. A chief of staff or a departmental chair should be able, if it seems to him (rightly or wrongly) that his superior is making a serious mistake, to tell him so courageously. But this sort of collaboration is really effective only if such frankness has true admiration and constant devotion behind it. If the lieutenant does not admit that his chief is more experienced and has better judgment than himself, he will serve him badly. Criticism of the chief by a subordinate must be accidental and not habitual.

Marshal Pétain tells that when a new officer was proposed for his general staff during the First World War, he took him out to the field, described a tactical problem according to the terrain conditions, and then himself indicated a solution. If the officer agreed with everything and proved himself to be what the Americans call a "yes-man," the marshal rejected him; if on the contrary he criticized the great chief's ideas respectfully but firmly, he was congratulated and appointed. "The trouble was," added the marshal, "that this soon spread through the whole army and I could not open my mouth without the humblest lieutenant saying energetically: 'No, Monsieur le Maréchal!' One day I was really mad with one of them and I had to send him down the earth . . . This was the end of the experience."

What must an assistant do if he is sure he is right and if his boss refuses to accept his criticisms? An administrator or an officer must execute the order after offering his reservations. No collective work is possible without discipline. If the matter is so serious that it can have a permanent effect upon the future of a country, an army, or a company, there is the option of a resignation. But this must be done only as a last resort; as long as a man thinks he can be useful he must remain at his post.

Sometimes a threat of resignation suffices, but it is a weapon that wears down easily. When Lyautey, as a young commander, first took orders from Colonel Gallieni, the latter taught him the art of resigning. Every time the governor-general of Indo-China refused to give an order requested by Colonel Gallieni the latter sent in his resignation; but since he was very much needed, the resignation was not accepted and his request was granted. When later on, in Madagascar, Lyautey had Gallieni as supreme commander, an argument arose between the two men an the younger sent in his resignation. It came back to him in a few days with these words written on its margin: "Oh, no. Not to me! Gallieni."

b) *Agility.* A chief of staff, a chief of cabinet, or an assistant has to adapt himself to the rhythm of thinking and the working habits of his chief. Occasionally the orders given are obscure; he must translate them. Foch's orders were translated by Weygand. Sometimes the chief's ideas are merely lighting bursts that momentarily illuminate the obscure future; the chief of staff must derive detailed directions from them. Thus, Berthier translated the Emperor's ideas into directions for the movement of troops. If the chief's mood is variable, it rests with the chief of staff to pacify those "humiliated or offended," or to warn visitors discreetly about subjects which should be avoided.

During the war, I was attached as translator of an English general. He was a brilliant organizer and fundamentally a good man, but so gloomy and of such difficult character that he was known by his officers as "The Black General." Due to a happy chance (and because I was French) I was not only spared his bad temper but treated with affectionate familiarity and invited to have tea alone with him every afternoon. In the course of our intimate conversations, I was able to tell him anything, and I gradually found myself (foreigner) entrusted with innumerable missions by British officers desirous, in the interest of the service or their own careers, of acquainting "The Black General" with facts which he would have refused to consider if the officers themselves had presented them to him.   I realized then the service one could render to both to individuals and the team when a powerful man takes us into his confidence.

A great man's manias must be respected, because the time spent fighting them is too precious to waste. A departmental head and his chief reach a state of symbiosis; the clever collaborator knows what words must never be spoken in the chief's presence because they stir up painful complexes and unleash his anger. He knows how to present a proposition that would interest and that would result in a favorable opinion from the chief. He is clearly aware of the errors and weaknesses of the chief, respects him no less for them, but he does his best to make up for deficiencies.

c) *Discretion*. This work of assisting a chief or a company owner puts young people, unaccustomed to responsibility, power, or the giving of orders, in close participation with deliberations and decisions of the most serious sort. Under such special circumstances, *secrecy* is necessary. This is a rule that admits no exceptions. The young man (or the young woman), anxious of being associated with important decisions, may be tempted to impress others with stories or anecdotes of their work, but their duty is not to speak of it. The possible damage of such indiscretion is unlimited; and on the other hand they will find that discretion has equally enjoyable pleasures.   Nothing could be more exciting than to be at the center of confidential drama, to know the truth, to discover the plot, and to let nothing transpired. Madame Récamier was admirable at this game. There was a time when she received the confidences of the leaders of opposing parties, of two men running in competition for the same office, and those of an author and his critics. Madame Récamier listened, offered sympathy, forwarded messages when necessary, but betrayed no one. Her role was merely the answering of a few questions, but it was useful, charming, and played deliciously.

d) *Efficacy.* An assistant must not only provide requested reports, but also those which may be required later. He must anticipate the stream of thoughts of the chief, prepare the way for their accomplishment. The collaborator gets rid of unnecessary cares, arranges small details himself, simplifies the small and necessary steps present in daily work. An efficient secretary is the perfect model of the assistant. Her role is not confined to taking notes and typing letters; she must also classify the jobs done, file letters and replies, find addresses, and turn herself into a kind of walking data base. She must possess all of the virtues of a department head, as well as those of a woman. Being a woman, she has intuition, she understands the expressions of big egos, and she projects a positive atmosphere in the office. At the same time she must not make her femininity too obvious, for the day the boss becomes too conscious of it the work would be the one to suffer. A difficult but not impossible balance to maintain.

3. — MANUAL WORK AND INTELLECTUAL WORK - THE HOUSEWIFE

For a long time, men regarded work as a disgrace and a divine punishment. "In the sweat of thy face shalt thou eat bread." Manual work and much intellectual work were left to be done by slaves. In Rome, grammarians and mathematicians were slaves. Later, the theoreticians wanted to divide men into proletarians and bourgeois; the proletarians were wage earners and the bourgeois lived on invested income and profits, but this is a confusing distinction. According to this, a bank director with a yearly salary of two hundred thousand francs would then be a proletarian; a little shopkeeper or a small landowner barely earning ten thousand francs a year would be a bourgeois.

Alain has given a definition which I believe to be, if not completely fair, at least deeper and more productive. He calls proletarians all those who live by their work, manual or intellectual, salaried or not; he denotes bourgeois all those who live by their speech. To him, lawyers, communist leaders, and beggars are bourgeois because they all earn their living by persuading others to pay them. Masons, mechanics, engineers, and good writers are proletarians because they do not need to persuade anyone; the quality of their work is sufficient to sell it. A big manufacturer is a proletarian if his money is earned through his technical knowledge alone; he is bourgeois if his success in the administration councils comes from his sociability and public relations with important businessmen.

From here, says Alain, two very different states of mind are born. The proletarian who works upon and transforms nature does not need to please but the power to overcome and he is therefore an unrefined man; he does not appreciate courtesy; he dresses, not according to the fashion, but to suit the requirements of his work. To Alain, the bourgeois is amiable; he seeks to say the pleasant thing to those from whom his living comes: constituents, audiences, or friends; his clothes do not shock. Kipling, in an admirable poem, has shown the strange distant relationship between the Sons of Martha who do things, build bridges, pave highways, pilot airplanes, drive trains, and the Sons of Mary who sleep on the soft cushions of their luxurious carriages, cradled by the work of others.

Any division of human beings into two groups, or as it is still said into "classes," is dangerous and on the whole artificial. A young son of a bourgeois may be, in his taste and behavior, a proletarian who is not happy but in the company of engines. An engineer may be a Son of Mary when he travels, and a Son of Martha in his factory. But it is nevertheless true that some are spared the hardest work, while it is the daily necessity of others, and deep hatred springs up in this way. Is it possible to remedy an evil as old as humanity? Revolutions have always failed to do it. They will always fail because they ignore the eternal man and the truest of all dogmas, that of original sin.

But it is possible that the progress of the machines, after having rendered the life of the workers more arduous and more monotonous, will end by bringing it closer to that of the bourgeois. The length of the working shift has already been reduced by approximately one third in the last century. Work requiring the greatest strength is and will be left more and more to machines. It is true that machines have abolished the work of intelligent and skillful craftsmen, replacing it with the tedious assembly line, but this is only a transitory stage. The assembly line will one day be run by robots. The worker, whose role will then be scarcely more than one of supervising, will become an engineer.

In the present study, the important thing to remember in regard to manual work is this: work, any work, whether simple or complicated, can be well done or badly done. There is a skillful and a nice way to dig a trench, and a foolish and ugly one, just as there is a serious and a passionate way to prepare for a lecture, and a negligent one. A typesetter may produce a mediocre copy or a remarkable one. It depends upon her technique, the care she takes of her machine, the symmetry of the headings, the page size, and the attention she gives to proofreading. If her purpose is to make her work a little better than required, she becomes an artist at once and she finds herself rewarded for her extra effort by a deep and lasting satisfaction. She has not done this additional work for a supervisor, but for her own satisfaction, for the honor, for her own enjoyment; therefore, she has done it freely. Any work done in good faith leaves the worker with a margin of freedom.

The pleasure of working may become so complete that it often succeeds in replacing all others. In my efforts to imagine Paradise, I do not come to conceive it as a place of eternal relaxation where winged souls do little else than sing and play their harps, but rather one of a study where I work everlastingly at some marvelous novel of infinite length with the joyful strength and certainty that I could so rarely know upon earth. The Paradise of the gardener is a garden, and that of the carpenter is a bench.

The housewife. An excellent example of the mingling of manual work and intellectual work is that of the housewife when it is done with love. A woman who runs her house well is both its queen and its subject. Conceives, and often executes herself, her own ideas. She is the one who makes work possible for her husband and children; she protects them from worries, nurtures them, and cares for them. She is the Minister of Finance, and thanks to her the family budget is balanced. She is also the Minister of Fine Arts, and it is her doing if the house or apartment has charm. She is the Minister of Family Education and thanks to her the boys get into the technical college and the girls become knowledgeable and refined.

A woman should be as proud of her success in making her house into a perfect little world as the greatest statesman of his in organizing the affairs of a country. Marshal Lyautey was right when he said that the question of scale was of no importance. A perfect thing is perfect, whatever its dimensions. The work of the housewife is the hardest of all, except in the very wealthy families. It is anything but relaxed. A two-day holiday from shop or workroom means two days spent in cleaning, washing, mending, and caring for the children. There is always something urgent to be done for a family. Add to this her preoccupation to look attractive, to dress properly, and to learn new things. Indeed a woman's job, if well done, leaves few moments of leisure, but it is one in which the work gives an immediate satisfaction. Nothing is more beautiful than to see how a clever woman, in a few days, with very little money and much love, can transform a shack into a paradise. This is the point of intersection of the art of working and the art of loving.

4. — THE WORK OF THE STUDENT

There is of course an art of teaching. The work of teaching is a difficult one; it requires a long experience. We realize this the moment we try to become teachers of our own children. A father is rarely a good teacher; either he thinks he knows things and finds his knowledge to be very superficial, or he knows but he explains badly, or he is too severe and impatient because teaching bothers him, or he is dangerously indulgent because he loves his children too much to judge them. It is from professional teachers, who have succeeded in this art, that we must learn its rules.[3]

---

[3] For more about this topic, read Alain. *Propos sur l'éducation.*

a) *There can be no teaching without discipline.* The first job of the student is to learn how to work. Before the training of the mind comes that of the will. This is why home-schooling is never very successful. Excuses are too easily accepted by the family: the child has a headache; he has slept badly; he has been invited somewhere. The examiner was unfair, the problem was improperly posed. A school makes no compromise and that is its virtue. I am even inclined to prefer the old boarding-school system. It has some serious drawbacks; it sometimes produces immorality and it is always rather severe, but it makes men. Children learn by themselves to find a place in a society; in a family they find these places ready-made and it is too easy for them. With rigor, and if the parents are dedicated, day schools are satisfactory up to the age of fifteen or sixteen. Between the ages of seventeen and twenty, freedom in a large city is fatal for the children.

b) *To amuse is not to teach.* The object of teaching is to erect a framework of elemental knowledge in a child's mind and gradually to raise the child to the level of adults in his time. Later in life, the facts taught by experience and new discoveries will add themselves to this framework. It is senseless to attempt to alter this natural order and to appeal to a child's mind by entertaining him with the spectacle of modern life. Teaching by means of picture, radio, and the cinema is in itself ineffective; these methods must not be used unless they become (and this is possible) the means behind some effort or excitement. That which has been learned without effort is easily forgotten. For the same reason, oral instruction which does not require any personal participation from the student is always rather useless. Eloquence slides in and out of young minds. To listen is not to work. Naturally this does not apply to the teaching of modern languages which must always include listening comprehension.

c) *It is important to give tests and examinations to the students.* From time to time we see parents and education reformers propose the elimination of secondary education. They are wrong. Without assignments and grades there will never be serious work. For the same reasons, it was wrong to eliminate the General Competition of Lyceums and Schools, which happily have been reinstated; they are a powerful means to give the good students the prestige they deserve.

d) *Elementary education is the most important.* Parents have the tendency not to give sufficient importance to elementary studies. They say: "My boy doesn't know how to work, but he is just a child; he is a seventh grader." The truth is that everything depends upon a few methods being well learned in the beginning. Knowing how to read, to write, and to count well is an enormous advantage. The majority of people do not possess this elementary knowledge. Many men read poorly, laboriously, with words failing to evoke for them at once the ideas they represent. Mathematics are found to be very difficult or very easy, according to the manner in which the fundamental concepts have been taught. Imperfect knowledge of the first principles of geometry and the rudiments of algebra makes it impossible to understand anything of what comes next.

e) *It is better to teach a few things perfectly than many things haphazardly.* It is absolutely useless to overload the curriculum. The object of education is not to produce technicians, but *good spirits.* To achieve this, a few subjects will suffice. "Latin and geometry shall be taught mainly," said Napoleon. Add a little history, a little physics, and naturally a great deal of the language of the country. That will be sufficient. In history and science, it is not important the student be familiar with the most recent discoveries and the most up-to-date theories, but that he understands the historical method and the scientific method. The relatively simple works of the early scholars will be clearer and more useful to him than the elaborate details of modern physicists. Teaching, wrote Alain, must be definitively slow.

5. — THE ART OF READING

Can reading be called work? Valery Larbaud calls it the "unpunished vice," and Descartes, on the contrary, says it is "a conversation with the most honest people of past centuries." Both of them are right.

The vicious reading occurs in people who find in reading a kind of opium that liberates them from the real world sinking them into an imaginary one. They cannot spend one minute without reading; to them, everything is good; they will open an encyclopedia and read an essay on water-color technique as voraciously as they will an article on firearms. Left alone in a room, they will go straight to a pile of newspapers and magazines and plunge into the middle of any column, rather than be left with their own thoughts for a moment. They seek neither ideas nor facts in reading, but merely the endless procession of words which prevents them from facing the world or their souls. They retain very little substance of what they read; they set up no scale of values amongst the various sources of information. As practiced by them, reading is completely passive; they hold the texts; they do not interpret them; they do not make any room for them in their minds; they do not assimilate them.

Pleasure reading is much more active. The novel lover reads for his pleasure, to find either beautiful impressions, or the awakening and exaltation of his own emotions, or the adventures which life has denied him. Another will read for the pleasure of discovering among the poets and moralists a more perfect expression of his own observations and feelings. Still another will read, without studying a particular period of history, for the pleasure of verifying the similarities of human suffering throughout the course of the centuries. This sort of pleasure reading is healthy.

Finally, work reading is the sort done by the man who is seeking in a book definite knowledge or material needed for the creation or completion in his mind of a structure whose magnitude he has conceived in general terms. Work reading must be done with pen or pencil in hand, unless the reader possesses an extraordinary memory. It is useless to read if we must reread each time we need to return to the subject. If I may cite my own example, when I read a volume of history or a serious book of any kind, I always write a few key words indicating the important topics covered. Underneath each word I write the page number where the corresponding passage is located, in case I need to consult it without having to read the entire book again.

*

*   *

Reading, like all work, has its rules. Let us outline some of them. *The First rule,* is that a perfect knowledge of a few writers and a few subjects is more valuable than a superficial one of a great many. The beautiful features of a piece of writing are seldom apparent at first reading. In youth, one should search among books as one searches the world f or friends, and once these friends are found, chosen, and adopted, one must retire with them. Intimacy with Montaigne, Saint- Simon, Retz, Balzac, or Proust is sufficient to enrich an entire life.

The second rule is that the great writings of the past must figure preeminently in our readings. Of course it is both natural and necessary to be interested in the writers of our times, for it is among them that we are likely to find friends who have our own cares and needs. But let us not submerge ourselves in the tide of insignificant books. The number of masterpieces is such that we would never be able to know them all. Let us trust the selection made in past centuries. A man may be wrong; a generation may be wrong; humanity is never wrong. Homer, Tacitus, Shakespeare, and Molière certainly deserve their glory. We should give them some preference over those who have not undergone the test of time.

The third rule it to choose our literary nourishment well. Each mind requires its own particular food. Let us learn to recognize which authors are *our authors*. They will be very different from those of our friends. In literature as in love, we are surprised at what is chosen by others. Let us be faithful to what is appropriate for us. We are the best judges of that.

The fourth rule is that whenever possible our

reading should be done in the atmosphere of composure and respect which surrounds a fine concert or a noble ceremony.   Reading is not to run through a page, interrupt to answer the telephone, pick up a book when one's thoughts are elsewhere, lay it down until the next day.   The true reader procures long periods of solitude; for some especially admired author, he reserves a Sunday afternoon in the Winter; he is thankful for a train journey which provides him with the opportunity to read a whole novel of Balzac, Stendhal, or the *Mémoires d'Outre-Tombe*.   He experiences an intense pleasure from rereading a favorite phrase or passage he loves (the Madeleine in Proust, or Levine's betrothal in Tolstoy), as the music lover does when he hears the magician's theme in Stravinsky's *Petrouchka*.

The fifth rule, finally, is to make our selves worthy of great books because in reading, like in the Spanish inns and in love, one finds only what one brings to them. The delineation of emotions interests only those who have experienced them or young people who await their flowering with hope and anguish.   There is nothing so moving as the spectacle of a young man who could endure nothing but adventure stories last year and has suddenly developed a great liking for *Anna Karénina* or *Dominique,* because now he knows what the joys and the pains of love are like.   Great men of action read Kipling, great statesmen read Tacitus or Retz.   It was a great spectacle to see Lyautey absorbed in Shakespeare's

Coriolanus the day after an unjust government took Morocco from him. The art of reading is in great part that of finding life once again in the books, and thanks to them, in understanding life better.

6. — THE WORK OF THE ARTIST

The work of the artist is at once like and unlike that of the craftsman. Both must possess a technical ability. This ability can be acquired only by the careful study of the masters and the patient practice of exercises. Naturally, a gift is necessary (Mozart, Byron, Hugo, Chateaubriand), but it is important to understand that a gift, left uncultivated, will remain sterile. I have seen Valéry at work; I have studied Proust's manuscripts. There is only patient searching, constant revising, efforts to discover the word which either expresses exactly the idea or, for mysterious reasons of symmetry and harmony, it is the only one that will fit. The writing of a score for an entire orchestra presupposes a complex musical education which can be realized, even in the case of a man of genius, only after long and painstaking work. In the highest and most spontaneous art there is a part of gymnastics and training.

Naturally, after long searches and work, the artist acquires an experience, a self security of style and touch, which occasionally enables him to do it with a speed and an immediate success when he knows exactly what he intends to represent. This seems miraculous to the uninitiated. Whistler laughed at Ruskin, who reproached him with having painted a certain picture in one hour. He was able to paint it in one hour because he had been painting all his life.

But the acquisition of this technical ability which is essential to the craftsman is only a part of the work of the artist. Valéry says: "A poem is not written with emotions but with words." In fact, both are necessary. From the moment we are dealing with art, we must get back to the firm idea of an order and a form imposed upon nature. Form is necessary, but perfect form without contents would not move us. Beethoven's symphonies have admirable form, but in this form the soul of Beethoven is imbedded: his thoughts, his suffering, and his joy. Racine reached perfection in form, but what would this be without Racine's own passions?

It is necessary, therefore, that apart from his technical labors, the artist (and in this he differs from the craftsman) lived, or rather, had lived. "Poetry is emotion recollected in tranquillity." We see therefore that the life of an artist must be made of three parts: a human, carnal, and sentimental part, which alone will teach a poet what men are like; a meditative and imaginative part (the artist is a ruminant who must endlessly chew the cud of his past life in order to transform it into artistic material); and finally a part of technical work. This last may be short: I know great writers who compose for only two hours a day but whose meditations, readings, conversations are merely other forms of equally necessary work. "*Die ganze Arbeit ist ruhig sein,*" says Goethe. (All of our work consists in being relaxed.)

Must an artist live in the world or apart of it? I believe this is a question with an impossible answer. Total retirement, natural to the Saint, is unhealthy to most artists. They work marvelously so long as there are materials at hand. Proust, secluded in his cork-lined room, set out in search of the lost past; if we were to adopt his rhythm of living (and if we had his memory), no doubt we should each find endless material in our past lives. But we could not reconstruct again the work of Proust; most of us need alternating periods of work and relaxation. Goethe has further advice: "Solitude is a wonderful thing when one is at peace with himself and when there is a definite task to be accomplished." We must, therefore, define our task before we seek the solitude to accomplish it.

7. — THE ART OF RESTING

The art of resting is a part of the art of working. A man who is tired and in a great need of rest cannot produce any useful work. We are all familiar with those horrible mornings after sleepless nights when our brains refuse to function. Then it would be futile to attempt to apply the principles of the art of working. Those principles presuppose that we are in command of our bodies and our thoughts. The human organism cannot live without alternating work and rest. The English "Week-end" system is a prudent rule of social hygiene. I have seen French ministries so worn out that they could not keep their eyes open, and yet they were obliged to make decisions upon which depended the peace of Europe. In such cases rest becomes a duty.

When fatigue is the result of physical effort, rest is not a difficult art: a man throws himself upon his bed and sleeps like a beast; but with intellectual fatigue it occurs that sleep may be denied to those who would need it the most. For these cases, there is an art of sleeping. Here are some of its secrets: 1. *In order to sleep, one must believe in one's ability to sleep.* Sleeping pills taken in very small dosages are particularly useful in contributing to this autosuggestion. 2. *In order to sleep, one must adopt a position such that bodily sensations are reduced to a minimum.* In other words, the body must be comfortable, in a mild, even temperature, and in complete darkness. 3. *In order to sleep, one must banish all thoughts of the present, which cause insomnia.* Therefore, it is healthy, if possible, to oblige the mind to consider the distant past where the causes of our anxieties did not even exist. Think about your childhood, adolescence. Recall images which happened long ago and try to visualize them with your eyes closed as colored spots begin to form. Little by little you will be transported into a peaceful and different world; you will fall asleep.

Another method, completely different but often effective, is to regard insomnia as unimportant, even to think of it as a fortunate accident, to take up a book or some piece of work and, without setting a time limit, wait calmly for the moment when physical weariness produces sleep.

It is often difficult to fill the leisure time of an active and healthy man. When he is not working, he is bored; he goes around the house like a caged animal and sinks naturally into vices, which are merely the means of getting numberless of vivid sensations with which to fill his empty hours. Modern civilization has increased the number of rest hours with its inventions and machines. We must learn how to use this time. There are several methods.

a) *Relaxation work.* By this, we understand that

certain occupations which for some represent work, for us are entertainment.   Acting, gardening, fishing, hunting, carpentry represent work for the professional actor, the gardener, the forest ranger, the carpenter, but recreation for the amateur, even if the latter indulges in them with the greatest possible seriousness; first, because the change in labor, the use of different muscles and nerves is in itself a rest, and then because the amateur feels himself liberated from his struggle with the outside world. He does these things at liberty; he knows he may stop whenever he pleases. He is spared the fatigue of compulsion.

b) *The playing of games.* It is an even freer form of activity, because it does not have as purpose the solution of real problems, but the observance of an arbitrary set of rules freely accepted by all the players. The chess player and the bridge player are not in conflict with the Universe, but with pure intelligence. From here, two elements of repose arise: the players know that the loss of a game is unimportant, and also that the interventions of chance are limited. The *moral benefits of sports* must be noted here. Respect for the rules is self-imposed by the players, because without rules games cannot be played. Such a habit, when it has been imposed to a whole nation and to several generations, tends to form citizens who respect the laws. "He is not playing the game," the English say of a man who is dishonest in love, business, or politics. *Civilization is*

nothing but man's acceptance of common conventions.
Many of these conventions are as arbitrary as tennis or
golf rules, but because they enable us to foresee the
reactions of those with whom we live, they substitute
courtesy for fear and sport for war.

c) *The spectacle.* Here we act via a surrogate. We
attend motionless to the actions of others. We are
interested in them "because nothing that is human is
unfamiliar to us." The emotions and passions depicted
in tragedies and comedies are our own. We live them
with the author. Why is this restful? Because in the
world of art, no decisions are required of us. A drama,
which evokes our emotions and could be our own,
occurs in an imaginary world and we know this. The
aesthetic level is far away from the ethical one, but the
drama distracts its audiences from the pettiness of life,
involves them in its deep and noble passions, and in this
way can greatly uplift and ennoble them. However, an
excellent truce to actual struggles would become
detestable if drama were to take the place of real life.
The cinema and the radio, taken in small doses, prepare
the mind for new tasks by distracting it. If taken in large
doses, they numb us. These are, even more than
reading, "unpunished vices."

d) *Traveling.* Any journey is restful, not because it
does not entail varied and difficult daily actions, but
because it removes us from our responsibilities. Except

in the case of official persons, the traveler lives for himself alone and not for a community or a family clan. A foreign country is merely a spectacle; in it we no longer have the continual awareness of our responsibility. All of us, from time to time, need a plunge into freedom and novelty. After that, routine and discipline will seem delightful by contrast. Periods of rest, on the other hand, can and should be brief. It is wonderful to discover how a few days of travel restore freshness to the spirit.

8. — CONCLUSION

The man who truly loves his work returns to it after the briefest rest with a curious and strong voluptuousness. When a man identifies himself with his job, the end of work seems like the end of life. But does he ever stop working? A man of this sort carries his problems with him. When a writer travels, he turns some imperfectly worded phrase over and over in his mind. Does he awaken in the night? A series of words comes into his mind. There he is discarding imaginary passages in the darkness of his room. The manufacturer away from his office, lost in any beach, takes up a pencil and paper and recalculates a price quotation on the sand. If he is within reach of his factory, he returns there on Saturday morning, though his workers and employees are absent. Randomly wandering through the empty workshops, he dreams about alterations, increased output, and more efficient methods of production. The farmer walks over his land on Sunday. "There is not a grove of a tree nor a herb plant without a reason, a story, and a destiny for him. He subjectively assesses the effect of the last rain and that of the groundwater upon his crops. The trails show him the roads winding between the fields, the difficult slopes or the hills; everything is eloquent of past labors; everything suggests new ones."

There have been incompetent societies and inhumane leaders which have resulted in men hating their work. It is a natural sentiment to be attached to one's labor! "Work keeps off boredom vice, and poverty." It is the remedy for all the evils of the imagination. "God blessed work!," my English colonel constantly said to me during the war of 1914. Without work we would have been very unhappy. There were plenty of reasons for anxiety. We were separated from our loved ones, exposed to danger, uncertain about the future. But how could we abandon ourselves to these sad daydreams when we were submerged in our work?

Yet the other day (in September 1938), when we were on the verge of the most horrible of wars, when we were assaulted by the memories of night bombardments, we could not find solace anywhere else but in our work. I was, then, lucky to be enlisted in military work.

Intelligent officials kept us busy and passionately engaged from morning to evening. Our busy minds, aimed towards precise goals impossible to accomplish, did not have room for loose fantasies nor strength for the galloping of the imagination. At nights we had to sleep because we were tired. That is how we spent the tragic week.

What is true for individuals, is also true for nations. If an energetic government formulates a work program for France, and if at the end of such program we see a certain renaissance or the hope of success, then the spirit of the nation will not abandon itself to vain fantasies; everyone will have the impetus to collaborate in a great and useful national project; the whole country will exclaim, what my colonel did in another time, "God blessed work!" And this, I speak from experience, is a vote that always wins.

IV
THE ART
OF LEADERSHIP

"Man, naturally ambitious and proud, can never find within himself the reason why another one must order him until his own needs will make him understand. The extraordinary accidents will make him conclude that, without a leader, he will fall pray of the strongest one, and that is how he comes to love obedience as much as his own life and his own tranquility."

Louis XIV

Men can usefully undertake and properly accomplish a common task only when one of them continually directs the activities of all toward the same end. This statement is self evident when actions which must follow a rhythm are involved. It would be useless for a team of men laying rails or a rowing crew to exert themselves if a foreman or a captain did not control their movements. *Every* non-directed collective action turns rapidly into confusion and disorder. All who have fought in a battle know the importance of a leader in command; and what is true of the army is also true of the dockyard, the factory, the newspaper office, the whole country. Whenever men are required to act together, there must be a chief.

From the moment the chief makes his appearance and leadership becomes forceful and precise, order follows confusion. During the war of 1914, it was seen how poorly led divisions that retreated and fell into panic, then became troops full of courage and resistance the moment they were taken in hand by a commander worthy of the name. The same nation, composed of the same men, will show itself to be either rebellious or disciplined, depending upon whether its government governs or does not govern it. Without leadership there is no military action, no national life, and no social life.

In the same way, throughout history, human societies have chosen leaders who, superimposed in a pyramid fashion, formed a hierarchy. Every time the order established by these leaders has provided a nation with security about its fate, the nation tried to suppress the hierarchy; every time disorder appeared again the hierarchy was re-established in a new form. When the administrative and military hierarchy which constituted the Roman state lost its power, its place was taken by a feudal hierarchy, after a long period of anarchy. When Russia suppressed its capitalist managers in its industry, an oligarchy of bureaucrats and technicians performed the same functions. This is the reason why revolutionaries, in spite of their promises and their aspirations, have never brought about equality to the land.   There can be and there must be an equality of opportunity, which is what Bonaparte called "the career open to talent;" *one can and must desire the equality of everyone in the eyes of the law; but one cannot conceive of equality between leader and led; one cannot conceive of a society without leaders.*

1. — HOW TO ELECT THE CHIEF

Humanity in the course of its long history has invented but few mechanisms for choosing its leaders.

a) *The hereditary chief.* It is the oldest method. No doubt it was soon used by the wandering tribes of antiquity where the oldest son succeeded the father. A society without the order of primogeniture was subjected to fights between brothers, frequently followed by schisms and debilitation.   In the Bible and in Greek tragedy we find evidence of such conflicts.   In an ancient and respected monarchy the hereditary transmission of power is accomplished peacefully.   Besides, the hereditary leader enjoys, in the eyes of his subjects, a natural prestige which is immense and precious.   The role played by the king of England, as mediator amongst the parties, is due to such prestige.   Napoleon perceived this so well that he aspired to found a dynasty.   He knew that a defeated king would still be king, but that the Emperor would be supported only by continuous victories.

In estates or businesses which have been controlled for several generations by the same family, we find a similar concept. Directors, overseers, and farmers, normally impatient of all authority, will submit to that of the head of the family. This is not only a habit, but it is also a perfectly natural feeling and fair reasoning. A father can hand down to his sons the traditions of leadership and loyalty to the family business. The hereditary leader, like the hereditary sovereign, feels himself bound to his estates by ties of honor which require sacrifices of him. We have seen beautiful examples of this in France during the long economic crisis we have just passed through.

The danger of hereditary power is that the firstborn of the reigning or the leading family may be a mediocre or even a monster. Must the nation or the business then be trusted to a man who is incapable of leadership? Evidently not. Also, in certain countries where power is transmitted by heredity, there have been exceptions when the chief seemed unfit for leadership. In England, many times, the order of succession to the throne has been modified by Parliament. In the United States, industrial leaders have taken special measures during their lives to limit the extent of power that might come to sons unfit to succeed them. Balanced by tradition and good reasoning, controlled by a parliament or a council, hereditary power has great virtues.

b) *The elected leader.* The first quality of a chief is to be recognized as such. Any questionable chief is a weak one. The elected leader should apparently have an undisputed authority over those who elected him. But it often occurs that the qualities which helped him become elected (eloquence, affability) are not leadership qualities, and that experience will reveal mediocrity and powerlessness in the elected one. In a heavily divided country, it may happen that the elected leader only represents a little more than half of the electoral vote. If the other half experiences aversion or even repulsion for the leader, the resulting situation may be a dangerous one for the country. Many times we have seen great nations giving in to doubt and despair because the leader elected by the majority did not inspire confidence to the country as a whole.

To designate a chief by election becomes very dangerous when the leader exerts his authority over a smaller group, rather than a country, and he must be re-elected at given intervals. How can he obtain the obedience of men whose votes he will be soliciting shortly? To elect by majority votes the executive of a company or the general of an army is to bring bankruptcy for the company and defeat for the army. All regimes have understood this rapidly and even the most democratic countries have renounced it. They have limited themselves to let the people elect their representatives: deputies, senators, governors who are (or should be) *controllers, rather than chiefs.*

c) *The professional licensure.* The licensure is the system of choosing leaders by examinations which if passed successfully, entitle them to diplomas and offices. This method was formerly used in China, and to a certain degree it is ours today. In order to be appointed for positions in the army, in the public works field, in the diplomatic service, and in most administrative positions, a French national must pass certain examinations. This method seems fair because the examination conditions are the same for all participants. It has, however, serious drawbacks: 1. Because the age when the aspirant takes the tests is not the one appropriate for leadership. A man who could have been an admirable leader at forty might find himself rejected for not showing early signs of these abilities. 2.- Because the qualities which make a good leader do not always appear and often they are not even recognized during an examination (Paul Valéry says, in good sense, that the greatest evils in our society are elections and diplomas).

The licensure system is *absolute* when an examination guards not only an admission to a career but also each subsequent promotion, which will be granted only after a new set of examinations. In France, this is the case with the medical profession. In the army, the École de Guerre and the École des Hautes Études Militaires constitute two additional barriers to be surmounted, but seniority, election, and personal favor play an important role in peacetime as victory does in wartime. The French system is a temperate licensure.

d) *Seniority and election.* There is little to be said about seniority. It is evident that when men grow older they acquire professional experience, unless they are completely idle, stupid, or too obstinate to learn anything, which is often the case. But there are many old men and no one has ever maintained that in order to discover the best leaders one merely has to look at the birth certificate. In other words, we must elect them.

The election of chiefs by leaders above, who would depend on their subordinates and who would be held accountable for their actions, appears to be the most reasonable method. The head of state (hereditary king, or elected president) selects a prime minister who must then be ratified by a senate or parliament; the prime ministers appoints his own ministers; each minister appoints his department heads; each department head appoints the various service jobs under his jurisdiction. The pyramid is built from the top down, which would be shear madness in architecture, but it gives good results in administration.

In fact, this system is as good as human affairs can be; it is wise in principle, but it functions in an imperfect manner. Apart from those of the president and of several political ministers, *all* appointments, including those which require scientific knowledge, should be based on considerations of technical competence and ethics. In the interest of the country, and therefore of those who govern it, the head of the army or the railroads should be the best qualified man for the job, whatever his political opinions, religion, friends, or connections. But nothing can prevent men from having strong passions. Friends and relatives and political relations play a part in appointments and this is sometimes regrettable. We must all try to control others and ourselves in order that merit may not suffer.

e) *The imposed chief.* In certain desperate cases when a nation is disorganized, no one appoints a leader; he imposes himself. No supreme power appointed Cromwell, who was a small and obscure land owner commanding a few cavalrymen. The Revolution made Bonaparte a general; he made himself the leader of the nation. Recent examples of this are in everyone's mind. It is evident that the leader who gains his position by force almost always has the necessary qualities for leadership; if he did not have them he would not have acquired so much power. The problem is to discover whether his virtues are those of a party leader, or can rather reach the level of a national leader. In the case of Bonaparte, the party leader was soon dominated by the head of state. Here came the greatness of the Premier Consul. If he did not always succeed, he did not cease to desire with less intensity to have become the man of the reconciliation and the supreme chief of all French nationals. "From Clovis to the Public Health Committee, I do not regret anything; I accept it all." When a self-appointed leader comes into power, the difficult question of his successor then arises. Cromwell's son did not rule for long; Bonaparte's son died in exile. Lenin's successor hated and destroyed his predecessor's work.

The truth is that choosing a leader is a problem which does not admit a unique and perfect solution. Everything depends upon circumstances of the past and upon the objectives the nation must reach in the future. But whether a leader is elected, appointed, imposed by birth or power, he cannot last if he does not possess the qualities that are required for leadership.

2. — THE QUALITIES OF A LEADER

The mission of a leader is to direct the actions of others; it is imperative that he knows the goal towards which he intends to lead them. Amongst all the qualities, the most important is *will power*, a leader must know how to make decisions and take responsibility for them. Naturally, before making a decision, he must inform himself thoroughly and weigh all of the elements of his decision. When he has decided and given his command, he must remain faithful to his decision, unless some unexpected and insurmountable obstacle is encountered. Nothing is as discouraging to subordinates as an indecisive and hesitant chief. "Firmness," said Napoleon, "prevails in all things." In September 1938, Mr. Chamberlain wanted to make peace and avoid war. One may criticize his policies, but even his own adversaries must recognize that, having decided on these policies, he made them successful because of his tenacity.

In order to make decisions, a leader must possess great *moral courage*. These decisions are frequently painful to him. At the beginning of the war, joffre was obliged to remove several generals who were his friends. Occasionally the sacrifice of a few men is needed in order to save many people. A leader can and often must be severe; he has no right to be malevolent, or cruel, or vindictive. He must reject idle gossip, but if possible he should align the public opinion in his support.

He must surround himself with a fully devoted *team* of people who can deal with minor decisions for him. He must not let the trees hide the woods. For the execution of orders, he has his technicians, whom he has chosen and in whom he has confidence; he allows them to act freely and is content to verify, by frequent checking, the accuracy of the information they bring him. "And you?," Lyautey was asked one day. "What do you do?" He replied, "I am a technician of general ideas." A leader with experience behind him knows that it is not possible to regulate in detail the activities of each one of his subordinates. In matters of economics, in particular, he confines himself to indicate certain general directives and to assure that private interests have respect for public interest; *he does not pretend to substitute by a plan the results of the desires of millions.* The traffic officer regulates the flow of traffic; he does not assign a particular course to each vehicle.

The chief must inspire the respect of his subordinates; if he cannot, there will be doubts and conspiracies. There is only one way to be respected: one must be *respectable.* A great leader is a great character; he is unbiased and without self-interest. Mr. Baldwin and M. Poincaré were perhaps lacking in brilliance, and Baldwin made a point of not having it, but they were both men whose financial honesty could not be questioned at all. Baldwin bequeathed a part of his fortune to the nation; Poincaré refused to use a government aide to deliver a private message. Both exhibited the simple qualities that an ordinary man expects from a good factory manager or a good husband. *These elementary virtues constituted their strength.* One could approve or disapprove their policies, but even their opponents did not refuse them the right to govern. A dictator gains power through being frugal and incorruptible. Boulanger had in his hands wonderful opportunities many times throughout his career; he was never worthy of his own fortune.

A leader must have but one passion: *for his work and his profession.* He must be reserved and even surround himself in mystery. It is not bad that he is the center of a legend. I would not criticize him if he guarded the development of such a legend. The character commands and governs as much as the real person. Kipling has described the Man Who Would Be King, as an adventurer who by the sheer force of his character dominated several mountain tribes and became their chief, but he lost his prestige and his throne one day when he was weak enough to fall in love with one of his subjects and allowed her to see that he was only a man. "How many men," said Napoleon "are guilty merely because of their weakness for a woman." And here we should speak about the leader's wife, who plays a difficult role; she must defend him against the world, keep him from fatiguing himself uselessly, refrain from suggesting impulsive actions, make her house a peaceful refuge and not another empire to be governed, the most ungovernable of all.

One day, during a discussion in the presence of

William Pitt about the essential qualities of a statesman, someone mentioned working abilities, another energy, still another, eloquence. Pitt said "No, the essential quality of a prime minister is patience." He was right, not only in regards to a prime minister, but to all those who will lead a group of men. Stupidity is an important factor in human affairs. The true leader is always ready to encounter it and prepares to endure it patiently, as long as it is normal stupidity. He knows that his ideas will be distorted, his orders poorly executed, and that his department heads will be jealous of one another. In his plan he accounts for these inevitable phenomena. Instead of seeking subordinates without faults, who do not exist anywhere, he tries to make the best use of the ones given to him. He leads men as they are and not as they ought to be.

Another form of patience is *constancy of effort.* When an objective is achieved, the true leader does not believe that his affairs and those of his country have been put in order for eternity. Nothing in this world is ever permanently solved. "The most dangerous moment," said Napoleon, "is at the moment of victory." If a garden, regardless of how well kept, is neglected for a time it will be invaded by weeds. If a rich and powerful country is left without discipline for a few years, it will be devoured by the bad citizens and later by its neighbors. A leader knows that one never reaches definitive results, and that each morning upon awakening he will have to re-start his work.

An equally necessary virtue is *discretion*. "Secrecy," said Richelieu, "is the soul of national affairs." Charles I of England lost his throne and his head because of an indiscretion. He conceived a plan to arrest the heads of the rebellion at the parliament in session, but he was imprudent enough to confide his plan to his charming queen, Henriette of France. Excited, she told one of her trusted ladies what was about to happen, and the latter, having friends in the other camp, lost no time in warning the threatened members. Thus, when the king made his move he found his birds flown and the people up in arms. *Moral*: "Never tell anything but what is needed, to whom is needed, when is needed."

"Nothing," writes Colonel de Gaulle, "strengthens authority as much as silence. To talk is to dilute thought, to waste passion, in short, to diffuse oneself, when what the action requires is concentration. Between silence and order there is sort of needed correspondence. 'Attention!' is exclaimed to the troops to alert them of imminent action. Since anything coming from the chief is contagious, he can provoke calmness and attention just by shutting up. . ." In *Rocrois*, the young and fervent Condé rides his horse, surveys the terrain, inspect the lines without saying a word. . . Hoche, forced to mature prematurely by his leadership role, is transformed from passionate and brilliant to cold and laconic. . . Was anyone so taciturn as Bonaparte? The Grand Army followed his example. "I have known officers," wrote Vigny, "who enclosed themselves in a monastic silence and who never opened their mouths except to give an order." Louis XIV had a grand and serious manner "which inspired fear and respect in public and prevented people whom he greatly admired from taking liberties even privately." No doubt it is very difficult for a leader to keep the right balance between the reserve and solemnity necessary to his prestige and the affability required for the coordination of his team. But this difficulty may be overcome easily by tact which comes naturally from those who are born to occupy great positions.

To all these qualities let us add *physical courage* , the only virtue which precludes hypocrisy, and *health.* Good health is a great asset for a leader. Then, patience, work, and will are easier for him. Two of Marshal Joffre's great qualities were his ability to sleep, and his appetite. To them we owe the victory of Marne, because good physical equilibrium assures harmony of mind. "Coolness is the most important quality for a man destined to rule." One recalls the occasion when Gallieni, after giving some orders on the battlefield, opened a book to read. Lyautey, then a young officer, was astonished at such an attitude. Gallieni said to him: "Since I have already done all I could do, I now wait for new results; while waiting, I think about something else." It was a good way of clearing his mind and maintaining his calmness. Lyautey followed his example later when, besieged at Fez and believing all to be lost, he asked that paragraphs of Vigny be read to him. "It gives me pleasure," said Montaigne, "to see a general before a stronghold which he intends to attack soon, giving his whole attention to free conversation surrounded by friends; and also to think of Brutus stealing a few hours from his nocturnal duties to read and annotate Polybius with the greatest security. Only the insignificant minds, buried under the weight of their own work, do not know how to put it aside and take it up again."

3. — THE INTELLIGENCE OF THE LEADER

Character is more important than intelligence, but intelligence is nevertheless essential. It is desirable for a leader, engineer, officer, or statesman to have *a broad education*. Poetry and history will teach him how to better understand human passions. Culture offers the man of action some solace to rekindle his serenity from time to time. Culture provides him with models of order and clarity. To reconstruct a country, to lead an army is, in certain sense, a work of art. He who has acquired a taste for beauty from his studies will be the more successful than others.

"If the value of scientific studies," writes Marshal Foch "lies in accustoming the mind to the consideration of materially determined magnitudes and formulas, the value of studying literature, philosophy, and history is to give life to ideas about the living world, and to re-create them, and that is why such studies enlighten and widen intelligence and in the end maintain it alive and fruitful in the realm of the undefined which life opens to us . . . The future will only increase, especially for a higher official, the necessity to acquire general culture along with his professional knowledge."

Naturally, professional knowledge is also essential. Some time ago, when I published *Dialogues sur le Commandemient,* I received a letter from Marshal Fayolle, who was an excellent and modest leader: "A leader," he wrote, "could be anyone who has character, good sense, and above all great general knowledge which comes only after long study. It has not been sufficiently stressed that many in the high command during the First World War were former professors in the *École de Guerre:* Foch, Pétain, myself, and many others. . . It was the first time this happened: professors had become high leaders of an army. This resulted from the essentially practical instruction offered at the *École de Guerre.* This instruction is founded entirely upon history and adaptation; there is a constant adaptation to the present conditions, via theoretical work in the Winter and field work in the Summer. . . You are correct in that the man who for years has solved a large variety of problems in military tactics does not find himself at a loss on the battlefield. The solution comes from the brain already formed with the condition, naturally, that some good minds kept the instruction along rational lines, assigning the proper role to the physical, the intellectual, and the moral components in war. Care must be taken not to neglect one for another; all are equally necessary."

The intelligence of a leader must have *simplicity*. Action is difficult when the mind is full of complex ideas and plans. In the industry, extreme organization may be as expensive as complete lack of organization. The means of transmission use all the power of the motor. (For this reason, small businesses directed by one man have an advantage over large ones because of their lower costs and the better quality of their products). A leader must have a few very simple ideas, acquired from experience and confirmed by practical application. In the interior of this rigid structure, the chief will hold precise knowledge to use in connection with a given action.

The intelligence of the leader must be *receptive*. He must know how to use the minds of others. "One must listen a great deal and speak little," said Richelieu "in order to govern a nation property." But one has to listen only to certain men who are known to possess solid information and accurate data. To know when to shut

up is excellent; it is not less useful to impose silence on
the charlatans.

A leader should have a *rapid* intelligence. Time is an
essential factor in all action. In many cases, an
imperfect scheme put into action at the proper time is
better than a perfect one accomplished too late.
Sometimes time is so important that it should be
considered as the principal element in the problem to
solve. An air transportation minister should not say:
"Given my personnel, my budget, and the difficulties of
this administration, how soon can I build five thousand
airplanes?" but, "Since I must have five thousand
airplanes by the Spring, what budget must I insist on
and what effort on the part of my personnel must I
require in order to reach this goal?" In the fashion
business as in that of war, in the administration of a
bank as in that of a newspaper, slowness can be fatal.
Here the chief thinks quickly and surrounds himself
with assistants who act quickly.

*Finally, a leader must account for both tradition and
customs.* To his eyes, the existence of both is a joy.
Amongst the elements he must use to build the future,
the most solid ones are provided by the past. He will
have to reshape and transform them, but he will refrain
from rejecting them. In an admirable story sometime
ago, Kipling showed how the River Gods punished the
Bridge Builders for having defied the ancient laws of

work. We men of the twentieth century are marvelously equipped for mastering the universe, but the universe has terrible ways of avenging itself, and the consequences of our acts are not always easily foreseen. During times of revolution, it seems that men triumph when they destroy the traditional structures of a country. But to judge correctly, one must wait for the end of the experiment. The French Revolution ended in a Restoration. The wise leader does not forget that the Sorcerer's Apprentice experience great distress in quieting the magic broom which his spells had set in motion.

4. — THE ART OF COMMAND

Whether he is a minister, an officer, an engineer, or a manager, the leader communicates with his subordinates in three ways: by the orders he gives, by the reports he receives, and by the inspections he makes.

The first quality of an order is to be clear. A reflection may be vague, a project always has something of the vision in it, but an order must be precise. All orders risk being misunderstood; an obscure one will never be understood. "To do a thing well," said Napoleon, "one must do it himself." This is not true, but the prudent leader assumes that no one understands anything and that everyone forgets everything. It is therefore not enough to give an order; one must see to its execution when giving it, and anticipate anything that may nullify its effectiveness. *Human stupidity and the malevolence of chance are limitless.* The unexpected always occurs. The leader who endeavors to eliminate the elements of chance and who protects the weak points of his projects against Stupidity, is more apt to impose his will than one who does not take these measures.

These precautions become less necessary when the leader succeeds in gathering about him subordinates whom his experience has taught him to trust. Every national leader has his cabinet, every military leader his personal staff. The team knows the character peculiarities of the chief; it knows how to serve him; it understands his unexplained orders at once; it sees that they are carried out to the letter. There are nevertheless few people in the world who can be counted on. It was said of President Wilson that he had faith in humanity but distrusted all men. The true leader distrusts humanity but has faith in a few men.

How should these men be selected? *One of the missions of a leader is to make himself familiar with the personnel from which he can recruit his team of people.* One of the strengths Marshal Pétain had when he took command of the French army was his former professorship in the *École de Guerre,* where whole generations of young officers had passed through his hands. Gambetta journeyed through every part of France to get to know the Prefects. A man who has the honor to govern a country must devote himself to discover the best elements and to place them to lead important offices.

Not only must he make use of the best existing elements, but it is his duty and to his interest to create new elements. This is what numerous political parties do abroad, and in England for example, the conservative party. It keeps an eye on the influx of young men to the great universities, hoping to find those who can one day be turned into statesmen. It also maintains a special school for their training. If they prove themselves particularly brilliant, the party obtains a seat in Parliament for them, where the Prime Minister endeavors to give the best ones some experience by making them parliamentary secretaries, then vice secretaries of State. The role of a party leader is the recruitment of a governing class; on the other hand, this is also the role of an industrial leader, and some of them have understood it as such. Le Creusot, for instance, has schools which are admirably conducted and where an impartial classification prepares each adolescent for the highest position for which he seems qualified.

It is frequently difficult to impose a perfect intelligence amongst the members of a team. The leader must not permit that each office acquires an attitude of a class or a local parochial sense, which would put it at war with other offices. Between the machine and the transportation divisions in the railroads, or between the first or second divisions in the army, it is important that the chief teach that an army, a factory, or a country constitutes a unique living body, and that any fight between one organ and another is a literal suicide.

It often happens that a group of subordinates who unanimously love and serve their chief well are jealous of each another and intensely fight for his favor. The "boss" must foresee and calm down these sensibilities, which might dangerously weaken an organization. As the experienced driver knows by listening to the sound of his engine that one of the cylinders is improperly working, the innate leader perceives that his team is inefficient and seeks the cause and a solution. The cause is often insignificant: a grain of dirt in a conduit, a shrug in the shoulders, which is in fact just a nervous tic, is taken as an insult. Lyautey had an instinct for these things. "Someone is feeling paranoid," he said, and sweetly but firmly he immediately pulled the reins on the rebel.

The leader receives reports on the morale of the team and its members and on the results of his orders. He should always distrust these reports. I once knew an old industrial leader who said: "All reports are false."

He was not wrong. Almost everything in them is exaggerated, distorted, suppressed. The only way to avoid deception with the facts is to go and see for oneself, from time to time. The threat of such impromptu visits is enough to make wonders. Suddenly reports become factual. Marshal Pétain relates that in 1915 assumed command of an army section, which had been ordered to attack for several weeks. Also for several weeks, the reports indicated small advances of fifty meters and, naturally, with heavy casualties. Distrustful of these, General Pétain showed up at the front line with a surveyors measuring tape, sketched the reported front line with a given date, measured the distance between this line and the actual front, and at once discovered that the reports had been falsified in order to please the high command, and that the said advances were little less than imaginary. The statistics submitted to the chief are almost always praiseful, or are presented in a way that support the conclusions of the writer.

A demanding chief may be loved, even much more than one who is indifferent or weak. *The best means to impose firmness in a group is to accept only those we truly appreciate.* Every man easily endures criticism when the quality of his character and his mind are out of question. To express our feelings energetically and suddenly is a wise policy. A strong, but quick, comment is less harmful than a hostile and disapproving environment. Subordinates must know that if they do not execute orders they will be sanctioned, but also that if the execution of an order turns out to be a disaster they will be covered. A true leader always assumes responsibility for his actions. Just as a king must be the protector of his people against unfair advances of the Great, *every supreme leader must see that employees, workers, soldiers, sailors, are treated with respect and justice by their immediate supervisors.* This is the most important role, because the duty of the "boss" is twofold: he must not undermine the leadership of his intermediate supervisors, but he must not tolerate abuses of authority. Naturally, there is no fixed rule which dictates the procedure to follow. The leader proceeds through this, like in all other things, walking the tight rope while tilting the balancing rode to the right or to the left to maintain equilibrium. In 1917, Pétain suppressed mutiny with a mixture of severity, justice, dignity, and affection, and this is a beautiful example of this equilibrium.

As much as possible, the leader must prevent discontentment and seek remedy to injustice before any complaints are filed. To achieve this, he must maintain close contact with those he commands. In other words: he must maintain a physical presence. He must go to the trenches if he is a general; he must arrive at the factory with his workers if he is an industrial leader; he must know his subordinates. He should exercise some creativity and, making an effort to represent everyone, avoid unnecessary suffering and conflict to those under his control. The secret to be loved is to love and to know the profession better than anyone else. Men accept taking orders and even desire it, as long as the orders are given *well*.

5. — THE ART OF GOVERNING

Governing and commanding are two distinct arts in times of peace. To command is to lead a group of human beings under discipline toward a definite goal. An army officer knows that he will be obeyed by his men, except in rare cases of serious insubordination. He also knows perfectly well what his objective is: the defense or the conquest of a certain territory. The head of a large commercial enterprise knows that he must produce a certain commodity at a given price and in certain quantities and that if he fails he will be ruined and his employees will be jobless. Except for certain periods of social unrest, the head of a large company is the lord, provided that he complies with the law. A dictator is like an army general: instead of governing he commands.

But the head of the government in a free nation must direct toward obscure and shifting objectives the actions of a group of people who are not compelled to obey him by anything except the fear of anarchy, a fear which is dormant in times of progress. He cannot make the least move without being criticized by an opposition, which is more severe when it desires to put someone else in his place. His lieutenants are not respectful subordinates; they are his equals and his eventual successors. In a democracy, the position of president of a council appears to the impartial observer as one of the most difficult jobs in the world, and when certain reprimands are read one feels tempted to ask like in Figaro: "Given the qualities required from a statesman, does the reader know any journalist worthy of being a minister?"

What virtues should we require of a man to whom we have entrusted the direction of our affairs? Above all, a *sense* of what is possible. In politics, it is useless to formulate great and noble projects if these cannot be accomplished, given the actual conditions of the country and the times. The movements of the people in a free country are at all times the resultant parallelogram of forces. The great statesman is one who appreciates precisely what these forces are and says to himself without ever being seriously mistaken: "I can just go so far but not farther." The statesman *does not allow himself to favor one class*, and foresees the inevitable reactions of the sacrificed groups. A prudent doctor does not prescribe to his patient medicines to treat temporary symptoms which at the same time would produce permanent damage to the liver; similarly, a judicious statesman neither appeases the working class at the risk of angering the bourgeoisie, nor does he indulge the bourgeoisie at the expense of the working class. *He endeavors to regard the nation as a great living body whose organs are all interdependent.* He takes the temperature of public opinion every day, and if the fever increases he sees to it that the country rests.

Even though he should fully appreciate the power of public opinion, a forceful and clever statesman realizes that he can transform it fairly easily. A statesman must have measured the capacity for *indifference of the masses.* They have their explosions of violence. Their protests are alive, but on the other hand legitimate, if the government forcefully brings poverty on them, takes away their traditional liberties, or seriously interferes with their sentimental or family life. But the masses allow themselves to be easily led by a man who knows where he is going, who demonstrates true sincerity for national interests, and who inspires confidence in them.

A sense of what is possible is not only the ability to recognize that certain things are impossible, an absolutely negative virtue, *but also to know that, to a courageous man, things which appear to be very difficult are in fact possible.* A great statesman does not say to himself: "This nation is faint hearted; the institutions paralyze everything." Instead, he says "This nation is asleep; I shall wake it up. Institutions are of the people's making; if necessary, I shall change them."

But above all, *it is not sufficient to state that one wants some changes, but to act on those words.* Mediocre politicians spend most of their time envisioning projects and preaching doctrines. They talk about structural reform; they conceive faultless social systems and formulate plans for perpetual peace. When we discussed the art of thinking, we said *that a project is never an action.* People at the street side café talk; they do not govern. In his public speeches the true statesman knows how, if necessary, to make polite bows to prevailing doctrines and to pronounce ritualistic phrases to pacify those who guard temple gates; in fact, he spends most of his time in determining the true needs of the nation. For instance, the statesman says to himself: "In this year of 1939, France must above all maintain peace, assure its aerial defense, deploy a new air force, increase production, and finally put finances in order." He endeavors to accomplish these definite and precise objectives via the most direct path. Does he meet an obstacle in his path? He gladly accepts detours. Vanity, intellectual pride, and a spirit for the system are terrible disadvantages to politicians. Some party leaders are ready to sacrifice the country for a doctrine or a set of principles. The leader, the true one, says: "Let the principles die before the nation does!"

Will his work be incomplete? Will injustices

prevail? Oh! He knows it well. Every complex action is incomplete. In the beautiful book by George Bernanos, *Journal d'un curé de campagne,* an old priest tries to make a young one understand that not even a saint could turn a parish into an honest group of people. To illustrate his point with an image, the old man tells the story of a Belgian sacristan who wanted to make the village church sparkling like a convent parlor. "Oh, the old woman was a hard worker. She endlessly cleaned, waxed, and polished. Naturally, there was a fresh coat of dust on the benches every morning, one or two fresh truffles on the rug of the choir, and spider webs, my god, there were spider webs enough to make a bride's trousseau." The sacristan did not lose heart; she swept and she washed. The moss began to creep up the columns. Sundays filled the church with dirt; and holidays finally killed her. "In a way," concludes the old priest, "she was a martyr; one cannot deny that. Her mistake was not in fighting the dirt, but in trying to eliminate it completely, as though such a thing were possible. . . A parish is necessarily a dirty place."

A continent is even dirtier, especially an old continent like Europe which has been invaded for centuries by mushrooms and ants, by bitterness and hates. President Wilson was like the old Belgian nun. He wanted to turn this dusty old planet into a federation of lawyers. It was an excellent idea, of course, but it was impossible to carry out, just as it is impossible today to resolve everything, to prevent everything, and to clean up Europe once and for all.

A great statesman, like a good housekeeper, knows that cleaning has to be done every morning. A quarrel takes place; a dispute emerges, like a new stain. He dissolves it patiently and, while is washing it, he thinks that another one will result as soon as this one is finished. Since he knows that with human affairs everything is imperfect and temporary, he will accept a settlement however imperfect and temporary. Term after term, peace will be renewed. Ten years, twenty years, and the task of his generation will have been done. Then the next one will begin its day-to-day existence.

6. — THE RIGHTS AND DUTIES OF THE LEADER

The right of a leader worthy of the name *to be obeyed*. A society that cannot respect the leaders it has chosen is condemned, for it will become incapable of action. A human community may, of course, prefer one hierarchy over another. In times of war, for instance, it is necessary to substitute the military for the civilian and when this is done there must be allegiance from all levels to the chosen leaders. Lack of discipline in the factory means ruin for the business, just as lack of discipline in the army spells defeat to the armed forces. Similarly, communities subject to two conflicting hierarchies are poorly constituted. It is a bad thing for workers to be torn between two disciplines: that of their employer and that of their trade union. The limits on the employer's and the union's power must be clearly indicated; and when this has been done, absolute authority should be given to each in their own sphere. Such an arrangement has been shown to be possible in England and in the Scandinavian countries.

The leader also has the right to last. How could he accomplish great results without the proper time at his disposal? Before entrusting a man with the reorganization of a colony or the establishment of an airplane factory, it is necessary to obtain all possible reports and to be quite certain that he is the best man for the position. But when the choice is made, he must be given the time to acquire some experience. Except in cases where it is evident that a mistake has been made and that the chosen man is unworthy, he must be kept on the job. Time establishes innumerable connections and facilitates the exercise of authority. When Lyautey was asked to tell the secret of his success in Morocco, he replied: "I spent thirteen years there."

But how can one reconcile discipline and time in office with the free exercise of the right of criticism? Would a leader with unlimited power not soon turn into a tyrant or a madman? Aldous Huxley invented "the Caesar game" some time ago; with each of his friends, he asked himself: "Which one of the Caesars this one would resemble if he were given supreme power?" Very few characters pass this test . . . And nevertheless criticism is necessary, but what part can it and ought it to play?

In the army and, generally speaking, in all cases where immediate action is required, obedience must be unconditional. Criticism should come only from above. On the contrary, during the normal life of a free country, the right to criticize belongs to everyone! It must be done within certain limits which experience has taught man.

It is good to change the leader from time to time, if such is the will clearly expressed by the nation. It is bad when he is defamed; it is also bad when he is changed too often, and inadmissible when the street pretends to impose him the laws. In order to establish true liberty, which is the greatest thing, there must be not only free institutions, but also good moral and ethical education. We will be worthy of becoming a free people in proportion to the way each one of us had learned to respect the legal leader, to accept the existence of an opposition, to listen to the arguments of the opponent, and especially to place the interest of the country above partisan passions and private interests. *Liberty is not one of man's inalienable rights; it is a desirable but difficult conquest, which must be asserted every day.*

This moral education is even more necessary for those who are destined to lead. The leader must have, above and beyond control, a strong sentiment for his duties. A leader cannot retain his position unless he renders himself worthy of it every day. He is not a leader if, having been placed as head of a group or enterprise, he only seeks to better his personal affairs. He is not a leader if, having accepted a commanding position, he puts his pleasures above his responsibilities. He is not a leader if, having to direct other men, he gives in to anger, resentment, or on the other hand to favoritism and nepotism. The role of the leading classes is to lead, that is to indicate the path of honor and work. *To lead is not a privilege; it is an honor and a responsibility.*

V
THE ART
OF GROWING OLD

"Few are those who know how to be old."

La Rochefoucauld

"An then, complete joy comes at dusk,
For those who traveled the path fruitfully."

Corneille

Growing old is is a strange thing, so strange that we often have difficulty in believing that it can reach us as it does others. Proust has admirably described in *Le Temps Retrouvé* the astonishment we experience when, after thirty or forty years, suddenly by chance we re-encounter a group of men and women who were adolescents like us when we first met them. "At first," he says, "I could not understand why I was so slow in recognizing the host and his guests; why they all seemed to be in disguise, mostly with dusty wigs that completely changed their appearance . . . The Prince himself seemed to have adopted the same regalia he had prescribed for his guests: he exhibited a white beard and dragged his feet as though they were in leaden slippers. His mustache was white too, as though it had the frost of Tom Thumb's forest upon it; it seemed to get in the way of his tightened mouth and he should have removed it after he had gotten his effect."

Later on, when he met one of his friends of adolescence, Marcel Proust added: "I met him at the atrium of my life, and to me he was my friend, a boy whose age I unconsciously calculated, since I felt that I had not lived since that time, to be the same as my own. I heard people saying that he looked like his age. I was surprised to notice on his face several signs that are, in essence, characteristic of old men. I understood this was so, because he was in fact old and that life makes old men of boys who live for a sufficient number of years."

Yes, it is only by observing the effects produced by time on men and women of our own age that we see, "as in a mirror," what has taken place in our own faces and in our own hearts. For in our own eyes which have come along with us through the years we are still young; we still have the fears and the hopes of youth; we do not imagine the position where young people place us in the generational scale. Sometimes a word offends us. A young writer addresses us as "Dear master," when we thought we were his own age, almost his fellow colleague. An even more painful experience: we hear someone says about a young girl: "She is crazy; she married an old man of fifty-five with white hair!" And we remember we are also fifty-five years, have white hair, and a heart that does not want to age.

1. — THE SHADOW LINE

When does old age begin? For a long time we thought we have escaped it. Our spirit remains joyous; our strength seems to be unimpaired. We run a few tests: "Shall I be able to get up that hill as quickly as I did when I was young? Yes! I'm a little out of breath on reaching the top, but my time is the same as it used to be. In any case, wasn't I always a little out of breath when I was young?"

From adolescence to old age, the transition is so slow that he who changes is scarcely aware of doing so. This evolution occurs via gradual transformations so slow that they escape daily observation, just as the Autumn follows the Summer and the Winter follows the Autumn. However, autumn advances, like the army that besieged Macbeth, concealed behind the barely discolored leaves of the late Summer drought. Then, one morning in November a violent storm tears off the golden mask and behind it appears the withered skeleton of winter. The leaves we thought still alive and green, are dead, clinging to the branches by a few thin fibers. The storm has revealed the evil; it has not caused it.

Diseases are the storms in the human forest. A man, a woman, seemed to us quite young, in spite of their age. "She is wonderful," we say, or, "He is extraordinary." We admire their activity, their mental sharpness, and the effervesce of their conversation. But the day after a night of excessive indulgence, for which a young man would have paid with no more than a headache or a cold, we observe that they are carried away by the tornado of congestion or pneumonia. Within a few days a face withers, a back bends over, a glance loses brightness. A moment has turned us into old ones. It meant that we had been aging for a long time.

When does this autumn equinox occur in our lives? Conrad said that when a man reaches forty, "each man perceives before him a shadow line, crosses it with a tremble and believes that the enchanted realms of youth are behind him thereafter." Today we would rather place this shadow line at about fifty, but it exists nevertheless; and those who cross it, as solid and alert as they may feel, experience the slight shiver and the brief moment of despair that Conrad describes.

"I will soon be fifty," wrote Stendhal on his trousers' belt (because of a strange attitude), and the same day he made a careful list of the women he had loved. Although he endowed them with all the diamonds of "crystallization" more successfully than any man in the world, they had been rather mediocre. At twenty, Stendhal had envisioned sublime amorous experiences for his life; he would have deserved them because of his knowledge about love and the importance that he attributed to emotions. But the heroines he dreamed of loving existed only in the books where he had brought them to life. As he crossed the shadow line, he wept for the lovers whom he had not had and never would have.

"I will soon be fifty," thinks the writer; and what have I accomplished? What have I expressed? It seems to him that everything is yet to be written and that he has scarcely glimpsed the books he should produce. For how many more years will he be able to work? His heart is not strong anymore. His eyes refuse to read at night. Ten years? Fifteen? "Art is long, life is brief." This phrase, which once seemed true but trivial, suddenly becomes full of meaning for him. Will he ever have occasion, as Proust did, to set forth "in search of the lost past?"

Old age is, far more than white hair and wrinkles, the feeling that it is too late, that the game is finished, that the stage belongs now to the rising generation. The true evil of old age is not the weakening of the body, but the indifference of the soul. What is lost upon crossing the shadow line, is not the power to act but the desire to do. Is it possible, after fifty years of experiences and disappointments, to retain the ardent curiosity of youth, the desire to know and understand, the immense hope inspired by the discovery of a new environment, the capacity to love without reservations, the certainty that beauty, intelligence, and kindness bond naturally, and the faith in the efficacy of reason?

Beyond the shadow line the mind enters a realm of even-tempered light, where the eyes, no longer dazzled by the blinding sun of desire, can see things and people as they are. How is it possible to believe in the moral perfection of beautiful women when one has loved one of them? How is it possible to believe in progress when one has discovered, throughout a long and difficult life, that no violent change can triumph over human nature and that it is only the most ancient customs and ceremonies that can provide people with the flimsy shelter of civilization? "What is the use?" says the old man to himself. This is perhaps the most dangerous phrase he can articulate, for after having said "What is the use of struggling?" he will say one day "What is the use of going out?" Then, "What is the use of leaving my room?" Then, "What is the use of leaving my bed?" And at last comes "What is the use of living?" which opens the portals of Death.

One may guess that the art of growing old shall then be to maintain some kind of hope, but before we can show this we need to describe old age in its natural state.

2. — THE NATURAL STATE OF OLD AGE

Except for the simplest organisms which escape death by dividing themselves into two new ones, every living thing comes to old age at a certain time in its life, varying with the different species. Why does the ephemeral insect have but two hours of amorous pursuit, while the tortoise and the parrot can live for two centuries? Why are three hundred years granted to a pike and a carp, when only thirty were conceded to Byron and Mozart? "Who can probe in God the unknowable thought?" The average length of a man's life was about forty years a hundred years ago; today, in the most developed countries, it is nearly sixty; a significant change, which allows us to think that, if wars and revolutions do not hinder the progress of hygiene, a hundred years will be the normal length of life in the next century; this, on the other hand, will not change anything at all.

The closer living beings are to nature the more cruel they are to old age. The aging wolf enjoys the respect of the pack so long as he can capture his prey and kill it. Kipling has described, in his *Jungle Book*, the rage of the cubs at being led into battle by an old wolf who is losing his strength. The day when old Akela missed his gazelle he was lost. The toothless old wolf was put out of his misery by one of his young companions.

Primitive men behave like animals in this respect.

A traveler in Africa described a frightened old chief who implored to him: "Give me some dye for my hair. If they notice that it is turning white, they would kill me." In certain villages of the South Pacific, relatives obliged their old men to climb coconut trees which they then shook. If the old men were able to cling without falling, they won the right to live; if they fell their cases were judged and their sentences executed.

This custom appears brutal to us, but we too have our coconut trees. Public lectures, conferences, and playing roles on the stage are tests after which the public may say of a statesman, an author, or an actor: "He is finished." In many cases this amounts to a death sentence, either because poverty comes with retirement or because sickness results from despair. War is the general's coconut tree. Young women are the slippery and dangerous coconut trees of lustful old men. A statesman who makes his ministers leap through burning hoops in order to test the flexibility of their joints is practicing coconut tree politics. In less primitive societies, old men are not put to death, but they are harshly treated. Montaigne relates terrible stories: That of the father who saw his son carving a wooden bowl and asked him what he was making. The son replied "It is for you to eat when you are as old as grand father." Another tells of a son who was dragging his aged father by the air to the door of the house, suddenly hears the old man shout: "Stop! I dragged my father only this far."

Among peasants where life is close to nature, it is physical strength that still regulates the relationship between the generations. In the urban realms one has to take into account the *age* of societies. During times of revolution and rapid change, the triumph of youth is certain, because youth adapts itself quickly and its reflexes are alive. During the French Revolution, youth understood the meaning of the war of the masses, while the old generation still fought the professional war. Today young people pilot airplanes as yesterday they drove automobiles. In these times of serious crises they cannot find before them, as was possible under well-established civilizations, acquired situations or powers of age and money. Today youth represents the only force; it upholds prophets who, proposing simple aims, offer them great and naive hopes.

Contrariwise, wealthy civilizations of long standing tend to become "gerontocracies." In these societies the old ones are in control of the high councils and cabinets, because in a world where no changes have occurred for a long time, experience becomes a precious asset. In a country like England, which gives great importance to precedence and is governed by tradition, longevity has the category of virtue. In ancient China, old men were the objects of chivalrous affection. "It is not right," said the Chinese, "that a man with gray hair is seen carrying a burden in the streets." The desire to please parents during their old age was a strong sentiment. It was a great sorrow to be absent at the time of the parents' death. In the public assemblies, only the old ones had the right to speak. They lived in their children's homes and they were deeply respected there. It was naturally expected of them to intervene in the affaires of young couples. A popular book studied in all Chinese schools stated: "In the Summer months, everyone must remain near the parents chasing away the heat and flies with a fan. In the Winter, the son must make sure that the parents' bed has plenty of blankets and the fire place is well kept; he must watch for holes and cracks in the walls, and leaks in the doors, so that they are sheltered from air and remain happy and comfortable throughout the season."[4]

These feelings and attentions are disappearing in modern China. In every young regime, strength is worth more than ancestral wisdom, but no government can remain young. As it grows older there is more respect for mature men; then for old men. The leader who has built his career based on the idea of youth, loses his own. Like the old wolf, he tries to hide his disgrace for a long time; he keeps himself physically fit; he has the courage and excesses of a young man; he displays an aggressiveness in which he no longer believes. But sooner or later time will make him a senator, then a corpse.

---

[4] Lin Yutang, *The importance of Living*

Thus "efebocracy" and "gerontocracy" alternate in a natural rhythm. What to do? All of the votes will be in vain. Circumstances dictate a solution. Rapid changes, new and strange inventions: the triumph of youth. Stability, established tradition: the prestige of old age. Perhaps the best scheme for the generations was that of Homer's warriors: several young heroes in active command of the armed forces; near them, the wise Nestor as minister of state.

3. — THE MALADIES OF OLD AGE

Here we have the social aspect of the problem. The problem is more complex for the individual. Old age arrives escorted with many difficulties. Are they insuperable? I do not believe so, but to overcome them one must face them directly. We shall try to paint a complex and dark picture of all of the evils that form the courtship of old age. During the development of this sinister overview, I shall ask my readers not to be afraid. We imitate the doctor who has a patient with a serious illness that requires certain precautions and says: "This is what will happen if you do not take care of yourself," and he then enumerates symptoms, each one more appalling than the last. "None of these will develop," he adds, "if you take the preventive measures I suggest." Here, then, is what the evils that accompany old age *could* be and what they will not be for you if you know how to prevent them.

In the first place, apart from exceptional people, an aging body is like a worn-out engine. If it was well cared for, inspected, and properly repaired, it can still give service. But in the end, it is not what it was: too many efforts should not be required of it. After a certain age, an action becomes difficult, manual labor sometimes impossible, and brain work of varied quality. Occasionally, artists remain in possession of their gifts until the end. Voltaire wrote *Candide* at sixty five; Victor Hugo created some very beautiful poems in his old age, and Goethe the admirable ending to his second *Faust;* Wagner finished *Parsifal* at sixty nine. In our own time Paul Claudel, at seventy one, completely rewrote *L'Annonce faite à Marie* which was first written in his twenty-fifth year. With others, on the other hand, inspiration comes to an end rather early, often because their talent was the result of youthful tribulations and because they never concerned themselves with the outside world. The silence of the heart determines that of the mind.

"Old age is a tyrant," says La Rochefoucauld, "who forbids indulgence in the pleasures of youth under penalty of death." First of all, those of love are prohibited. An old man, or old woman, can no longer inspire love from a young one. Regardless of how untouched the heart of the old person is, or how fresh the face looks, or how vigorous the body remains, it is very difficult, if not impossible, that a relationship in such a couple be as harmonious as that between two people of similar age. We could cite glorious examples: Goethe and Bettina, but Goethe was not the lover of Bettina and, on the other hand, one should ask how great a part is played by respect, admiration, and abnegation in affairs of this kind. Recall the admirable and cruel verses in Baudelaire:

"Angel full with beauty, you know the wrinkles,
And the passion of age. And the appalling torment
Of perceiving the secret horror of devotion
In eyes where a long time drank our avid eyes?
Angel full with beauty, do you know the wrinkles?"

Balzac has often described the tragic spectacle of an old man in love. Since he can no longer obtain the appreciation he used to win from his personal charm, except for gifts and endless favors, the aged lover will ruin himself for every young woman clever enough to awaken a crazy hope in his heart. Like Baron Hulot, he wanders begging for a favor to the point of disgraceful humiliation. Chateaubriand, who knew only too well what such suffering was like, left a terrible manuscript: *Amour et Vieillesse*, a long and grievous lament of a lover who does not know how to grow old. "The punishment of those who have loved women too much is to love them forever." And the punishment of women who have loved men too much is to hear the younger among them sometimes say with genuine surprise: "It seems like she was once beautiful."

In many cases the heart itself grows old. When it reaches the old age, it withers like strange dehydration. Could it be that there is a lack of physical desire, which provides a natural strong support to passions? Could it be that a realization of the briefness of life has weakened desire and affection? In any case, the egoism of certain old men is always surprising. Aphile spent his whole life with Eunice. He became her lover when she was twenty-seven. He incited her to leave her husband, and if he did not marry her, it was because he was himself married. She sacrificed her family, children, respectability, and friends. She devoted herself to his pleasure, his work, and his career. Their love affair was followed by a long friendship. When he was eighty and she was seventy, they were still meeting every day. Finally she died, and everyone who knew them was sorry for Aphile. "This will kill him," they said. Absolutely not! He experiences sudden rejuvenation. He was not only too old to love, but also too old to suffer.

This egoism of old age prevents many friendships. Younger people do not find the warmth in older ones which, combined with the experience of old age, would attract them. Stinginess is also one of the maladies of age. It has partly to do with a fear of being in want. The

old one knows it will be difficult to make a living and
that hard work may be painful to him. Thus, he clings
to what he has. He anticipates every eventuality: he has
innumerable hiding places and triple-safe boxes. But
fear is not the only reason behind stinginess. Every
human being needs a passion and this one is accessible
to all ages. It apparently affords keen pleasures:
counting one's money, investing it, following the highs
and lows of the stock market, dealing with precious
stones, keeping a little power despite a weakening body.
Stinginess becomes a game whose devotees can obtain
extraordinary delights by gradually eliminating, one by
one, all reasons for spending. In connection with this,
reread *Eugénie Grandet.*

"It is not the need of money," says La Bruyère, "nor
the fear of being one day in want of money which makes
old men stingy, for there are many such who have so
much money that they could hardly be anxious on that
score. And in any case, how could they be afraid of
losing the conveniences of life when they voluntarily go
without them in order to satisfy their stingy impulses...?
Rather, this vice is due to age and to the complexion of
old men, who give in to it as naturally as to pleasures in
youth or ambition in maturity . . . Stinginess requires
neither vigor, nor youth, nor good health. All that is
needed is to keep one's money in safety boxes and
deprive oneself of everything. This is convenient to old
men, who need to have a passion because they are

men..."

Faults of the mind increase with old age as do those of the face. Now incapable of taking up new ideas because he no longer has the power to assimilate them, an old man clings with crabbed tenacity to the prejudices of his mature age. Walking on the stilts of experience, he believes he is able to deal with any problem. Contradiction infuriates him, and he regards it as lack of respect. He exhibits the stubbornness and anger of a child. "In my days," he says, "it was not allowed to contradict an older man." He forgets that in his day these same words were spoken to him by his grandfather. Unable to interest himself in anything that happens around him, and therefore unable to keep himself up to date, he tells stories of his past over and over again. These anecdotes were charming in his youth; after an infinite number of repetitions they end up poisoning the following generations. If the younger ones listen to him, they yawn or exchange laughs and soon they will avoid him altogether. from here follows solitude, which is the greatest evil of old age. One by one lifelong friends and relatives disappear and they cannot be replaced. Little by little the desert widens around the old man. He would desire death if he did not fear it so much, even more as it gradually comes closer and appears so curiously threatening.

Tolstoy, who was an artist of great precision,

paints towards the end of *War and Peace* an surprising portrait of a woman who did not know how to grow old:

"After the recent loss of her husband and her son, she felt herself unexpectedly forgotten in this world without aim or object. She ate, drank, slept, sat up, but she did not live. Life left no impression upon her. She asked nothing from life, except repose, and repose she could find only in death. But awaiting death she had to live, that is, use all her vitality. She exhibited in high degree what is typical of very young children and of very old people: an outward purpose in life could not be seen; she merely displayed a capacity to exercise her functions and aptitudes. She felt the necessity to eat, to sleep, to think, to cry, to speak, to work, to lose her temper, etc. . . simply because she had a stomach, a brain, muscles, nerves, and a liver. All this she did without any driving external motivation, not as people in the full vigor of life do, when above and beyond the aim for which they are striving is the unnoticeable object of putting forth their strength. She talked because she had the physical need to exercise her lungs and tongue. She cried like a child simply because she needed to blow her nose.

"And thus in the mornings she felt the need to be upset, especially if she had eaten something heavy before, and she took it as a pretext Mrs. Biélova's deafness. . . Another pretext was the snuff, which she sometimes found dry, moist, or poorly cut. After all of these arguments, her bile rose to her face, and her servants could guess when Mrs. Biélova would be deaf again, the snuff moist, or the face of her lady yellow. Just as with the need to circulate the bile, she felt the need to use whatever thinking ability she had leftover, and she used it in some hobby. Did she need to cry? She started to talk about the defunct Count.

"When she felt the need to worry, the pretext was Nicolas and his health; when she needed to torment someone, she took it on the Countess Marie; when she needed to relief her throat from stiffness (which normally occurred around seven in the evening after dinner), her pretext was to retell over and over the same story to the same listeners.

"All of her relatives noticed the state of affairs with the old lady, although they never commented anything about it and everyone thrived to satisfy her wishes. Only by means of a few infrequent glances, half smiles and sad gestures did Nicolas, Pierre, Natacha, and Countess Marie exchanged expressions of understanding and preoccupation about her condition.

"But this glance had an additional meaning: it implied that the old lady had fulfilled her mission in this life, that it was not in what one could observe from her now, that they too will one day become like her, and that it was a satisfaction to obey and please this miserable

one, who used to be loving and full of life. *Memento mori*
this glance seemed to say.

"Amongst the people in the house, only the fool,
the mean, or the young ones did not understand and
avoided her."

Let us summarize the dangers of old age.   It
diminishes our strength; it takes away our pleasures one
after the other; it withers the heart as well as the body;
it separates us from adventure and friendship; and
finally it is shadowed by thoughts of death.

A very dark picture.

4. — IS IT POSSIBLE NOT TO AGE?

The art of growing old consists of struggling
against these evils and of making life's end happy
despite them.

Fighting our own evils. . .? But is this possible
when they attack the body? Is not old age a natural
physiological change, the inevitable progression of which
must be accepted? We have compared it to the aging of
leaves, which is the Autumn. Could not one write the
fable, *The Tree that Wanted to Keep its Leaves?* In vain
the tree would attempt to hold them, to fasten them, to

sew them to its branches. At the right time, the Winter storms will turn the tree into a black skeleton like its neighbors.

Nevertheless, civilization and experience have taught men how to struggle, if not against old age itself, at least against the appearance of it. Adornment plays a major role here. Aging women often attach more importance to their clothes and jewelry than do young ones. Nothing could be more natural. Bright jewels attract the gaze and turn it from the wearer's physical shortcomings. The soft lunar iridescence of a fine pearl necklace causes one to forget the wrinkled neck which it encircles. Sparkling rings conceal the age of hands, and glittering bracelets that of wrists. Pins, anklets, and earrings, just like tattooing in primitive tribes, dazzle the eye so that wrinkles and crows' feet may not be noticed. Everything that tends to make it difficult to distinguish youth from age is an act of civilization. The most refined age in history invented the wig, which was a homage rendered by hair to baldness. The effect of powder and blush is to make young women look like their grandmothers, and unwell women like healthy ones. The mission of fashion designers and beauty shops should be that of creating styles which would make it possible for aging women to keep hoping. After a certain age, the art of dressing consists of hiding one's shortcomings, and this is another form of politeness. The veil is a marvelous invention for blurring the image and transforming its wearers into unreal beauties. This means that all adornments are veils. They conceal the ravages of time as well as possible.

Will science be able one day to prevent old age from undermining and destroying our bodies? Will it create a true Fountain of Youth? It has often been said that the age of a human being is indicated, not by his birth certificate, but by the condition of his arteries and his joints. A man of fifty can be *older* than one of seventy. It must then be possible to make a man younger by means of a physiological restoration of his cells. Biologists have accomplished this with inferior organisms. Take a simple organism, for example some fish who live in the Atlantic. Place one of these in a small quantity of sea water and let it poison itself with its own excrement; it will age rapidly. Change the water every day; the aging process will stop. It is possible that the aging of our cells may be due to an accumulation of waste matter and that by a regular cleansing, we can lengthen our lives.

The rejuvenation of men and animals has been attempted by transplanting certain organs or injecting certain hormones. Old rats thus treated recapture their vigor, grace, and sexual activity. The effect lasts for about a month and the procedure has been repeated up to four times. In this way, a rat's life is lengthened by a half, and with an apparent increase in enjoyment.

However, the effects of this treatment are progressively shorter in duration and the aging faster. Doctor Voronoff's experiments with rams are well known. The results with human beings are less certain, but all this seems of little importance because any man today may reach eighty or more years simply by living a healthy life. Do we want to live longer than that?

In eighty years everything has been seen: love, and the end of love, ambition and the futility of ambition, two or three doctrinal insanities and their cure. Fear of death is not very great any longer. Affections and interests are directed to people who have died and to events of the past. "I am alone now and I make myself the object of a myth," said Goethe. In a cinema theater, when the show is continuous, the spectator has in theory the right to see the movie over and over again from the morning through the evening. In fact, when the scenes he has already witnessed reappear on the screen, boredom forces him out of his seat. Life is a continuous show. The same "fashionable" events take place every thirty years and they become boring. That is how the spectators get up and leave one after another.

When H. G. Wells was honored by a gathering of English authors on his seventieth birthday, he gave a speech in which he said that the occasion reminded him of his feelings during childhood when his nurse said to him: "Little Master Henry, it is time to go to bed." A child protests when bedtime comes, but deeply inside he feels that fatigue invades him and that rest will be something quite desirable. "Death," continued Wells, "is a nurse both affectionate and firm; when the time comes, she says to us: 'Little Master Henry, it is time to go to bed.' We protest a little; however, we know quite well that the time for rest has come and, deep in our hearts, it is this repose that we aspire."

5. — IS IT POSSIBLE TO AGE WELL?

If we accept without too much sadness the idea that life's span is limited, at least we would wished to reach the end of our journey with healthy minds and bodies. Is this possible? Quite possible.

Old age is not *necessarily* accompanied by the numerous evils we already mentioned. Observe animals. Many of them pass without profound physical changes from life into death. A well-exercised body will keep its flexibility and grace for a long time. The secret is to never neglect ourselves. What was done yesterday may be done today, and what is discontinued is lost for ever. Exercise and regularity can accomplish wonders! Many people of seventy fence, box, swim, or play tennis. The wise course is to keep exercising to the end, but not satisfy a whim or intermittently. It is not possible to interrupt the progress of old age once it has begun. To deny old age the possession of our bodies is fairly easy and infinitely desirable. "It is greatly easy," said Montaigne "to prevent and prolong human debilities. I prefer being old for a long time to being old before my time."

Therefore, there must be no premature physical renunciation. And there must be no emotional renunciation. The heart, like the body, needs exercise. Naturally, this is not about awakening feelings deliberately. But why, merely for reasons of age, should one deny oneself those that can be genuinely experienced? Because old people in love are ridiculous? But they are ridiculous only when they forget that they are old! There is nothing ridiculous about an old couple truly in love. Each one still finds in the other those qualities which were admired in youth. Courtesy, tenderness, affection, and admiration have no age. In fact it often happens that, when youth and its passions have vanished, love relations which were once imperfect, when they age, acquire a pure flavor, austere and delicious. Sensual misunderstandings disappear at the same time as sensuality; jealousy dies along with youth; aggressiveness declines with the body's strength. From the remnants of two stormy youths may be created a charming old couple. The life of a couple resembles a river which leaps dangerously and turbulently near its source, but whose clear waters flow more slowly as it approaches the sea, its broad surface reflecting the poplars along its banks and the stars at night.

The loves of old age can be just as genuine and just as sincere as those of youth; they have the purity of friendship and the ardent anxiety of tender love. Victor Hugo tells how deeply he was affected when he saw Madame Récamier blind besides Chateaubriand paralyzed. "Every day at three o'clock Monsieur de Chateaubriand was carried to Madame Récamier's bedside. It was very moving. The woman who could see no longer sought the man who could no longer feel; their hands met. God be blessed! They were close to death; they still loved one another." Faithfulness defies age. Disraeli dragged himself every afternoon into society to see Lady Bradford. The messengers were placed at the service of his lady. "They can wait all day in your house and be the slaves of your will." She undoubtedly caused him a certain amount of suffering, but for a romantic incapable of living without a novel, it was the pretext of his last dreams. Women should use their coquetry to stir up old mens illusions and fill their last days with the naive cares of adolescence. How many times we have seen emotional lives, believed extinct forever, brighten up with a surprising flare, like those wooden fires believed to be dead that suddenly flame up triumphantly!

Emotional life, moreover, does not consist of amorous impulses alone. Far from it. An old man's affection for his grandchildren can frequently fill his whole life.   It is delightful to watch our sons and daughters living their lives. We enjoy their pleasures, suffer when they suffer, love their loves, take part in their struggles. How can we feel left out of the game while they are playing it in our place? How can we believe ourselves deprived of pleasures when they are enjoying them? After our own joy at first going to the circus, is it not the most delightful that of taking our children to see it for the first time? After our pleasure of discovering by ourselves the poets we love, is it not the most satisfying that of seeing in the face of our children the admiration and joy they experience in reading the books we chose for them? And when wealth can no longer offer us great joys because our age prevents, is it possible to imagine a keener pleasure than that of using such wealth to brighten up in pleasure the eyes of our children?

It occurs frequently that relationships between grandparents and their grandchildren are stronger than between parents and their children. An old man, having retired from business,   regains the vivacity and availability of childhood. He is ready to play, tell stories, and listen to confidences; even a child's strength is similar to his own. While he can no longer run with his son, he can totter with his grandson. Our first and last steps have the same rhythm; our first and last walks are similarly limited. Nor is it true that an old man should be necessarily lonely. He will be, if he is self-centered, stingy, domineering, or feeble-minded; but if he fights against the usual faults of old age and is determined to be generous, modest, and affectionate, then he will see young people seeking his friendship and anxious to benefit from his experience. The difficulty for the old one will be to communicate this experience (which is always, if not disillusioned, is at least undeceived) without diminishing the natural enthusiasm of youth. After all, experience does not teach us that every enthusiasm is absurd. It teaches us to expect great results, not from great speeches and high-sounding words, but from hard work and great courage. This is a teaching that youth will accept from men who are worthy of giving it. It was beautiful to see Lyautey, at eighty, surrounded by a faithful team of youngsters, who came to aks the old chief encouraging reasons to keep believing and waiting. The visit to Meredith, to Mallarmé, to Bergson has always enriched the visitor with ingenious and noble ideas. A tireless old person is not a friendless one. Every year, toward the middle of December, I proceed by way of La Turbie on its high ridge, to a little house, like those of the Roman peasants, where M. Gabriel Hanotaux lives. Overhanging the sunken road, an olive tree, two thousand years old, evokes Virgil. Under the orange trees, the owner of the orchard climbs the steep slope more quickly than the young ones, in spite of his eighty-five years. His voice is full of flavor. "I speak," he says, "the French of the time of Louis XV. My grandmother taught it to me, and she learned it from hers."

M. Hanotaux's common sense is, like his accent, both ancient and young. "I shall give you a few precepts," he says "you should repeat whenever you are in need of comfort. They are simple and effective. Here they are: *"Everything comes . . . Everything is forgotten . . . Everything works out . . . No one understands anything about anything . . . If everyone knew what everyone said about everyone, no one would speak to anyone . . ."* This last maxim, which I love, has comforted me of many unpleasant rumors. M. Hanotaux adds: *"Above all things, never be afraid. The enemy who forces you to retreat is himself afraid of you at that very moment."* Here we have an old man whom the study of history and a long life have taught, not despair and indifference, but self-confidence and serenity. At eighty-five, he plans innumerable projects for the future; he considers several long journeys; he builds and he plants. In a similar manner, when the *Exposition Coloniale* was ended, Marshal Lyautey said to me: "And what am I going to do now?" When I told him "M. Marshall, the government will surely find some way of using you . . . ," he replied, "It will find, it will find! My dear friend, all this sounds very nice, but I will soon be eighty-one; if I am going to begin a new career I must get started."

That is the proper attitude. We have said "old age is the feeling that it is too late, that the game is finished, that the stage belongs now to the rising generation. The true evil of old age is not the weakening of the body, but the indifference of the soul." We can and must struggle against this indifference. Men who age less quickly are those who maintain valid reasons for living. It might be easily believed that a man is worn out and depleted by an agitated existence, violent emotions, struggles, studies, and endless seeking. As a matter of fact, the reverse seems to be true. Clemenceau and Gladstone, both of whom held the office of a prime minister when they were over eighty, possessed astonishing vitality. Aging is no more than a bad habit; a busy man has no time to acquire it.

But how can a man stay busy? When he grows old, are not occupations difficult to find? Furthermore, is it good for a country, for a business, to keep him at the head? The answer is that in many cases old men are better leaders than young men. It was the old Fabius who saved Rome. In the war of 1914, both sides were led by generals of advanced age. "Agamemnon did not want ten partners like Ajax, but like Nestor, and he was sure that if he had had them Troy would not have fallen that soon." An old diplomat, an old doctor, are full of experience and wisdom. Relieved from the passions of youth, they judge business and doctrine with fairness and serenity. "Great things are not accomplished with physical strength and agility," says Cicero, "but through consultation, authority, and the mature wisdom which old age, far from lacking, is endowed with abundantly."

6. — TWO DIFFERENT WAYS TO AGE WELL

In summary, there are two satisfactory ways of growing old. The first one is not to grow old. We have described it: it is the way of men who escape old age by living active lives. This is the meaning of the Faust myth, completed by Goethe at the end of his poem. In vain has the aged Faust regained a youthful appearance. Love, pleasure, and ambition have deceived him, but in the end work saves him. Near death and blind, Faust sets himself the task of draining a stagnant lake and turning what was a fetid swamp into a pasture for men and their cattle. "Yes," he says, "I vow to devote myself completely to this idea. Only he who knows how to conquer each day is worthy of life and liberty! . . . If I could exercise a free activity, on a free land, in the bosom of a free nation! Then I would exclaim at each passing moment: 'Oh, wait! You are so beautiful! . . .' Presaging such a sublime felicity, I rejoice at the present ineffable instant." At this moment Fausto falls dead. Everything has been fulfilled. Mephistopheles prepares to drag to his hell the soul that was sold to him, but angels descend and carry the immortal part of Faust to heaven, the part of him which never lost faith in the efficacy of action and for this faith he was granted salvation.

The second way of growing old properly is to accept old age. This could be a time of serenity, of renunciation, and therefore of happiness. The time for struggling is past, the game has been played, death's refuge is approaching, misfortunes cannot prey on us. When the aged Sophocles was asked whether he still enjoyed the pleasures of love, he said: "May the gods keep me from them! I have freed myself from them as from a cruel and savage master." I have encountered several old men who were like the wise men of our dreams. Released not only from the frenzies of love, but also from the responsibilities of a long-term future, they do not envy young people; they feel compassionate about the young ones because they still have to overcome the stormy sea of existence. Deprived of a few pleasures which they barely miss, they keenly enjoy those that remain. They know how useless advice can be and realize that everyone must live his own life. We are glad to listen to their recollections because they spare us their criticism, and when things become too difficult, we even ask them to resume their leadership. This we do it more readily because everyone knows that they do not wish this power.

There are more than two unsatisfactory ways of growing old. The worst is to be continually grasping at what cannot be retained. Everyone has seen the aging businessmen who refuse to delegate any of their power and who maintain their sons in a kind of disdainful slavery; the latter would love and respect them if they had the wisdom to share their responsibilities. We also know those close-fisted parents who force a son or a daughter to live mediocre lives in order that they may cling with their own trembling hands to symbols of the pleasures they can no longer enjoy; and we also know those ambitious old ones who, days before their death, poison their last hours with jealousy and repugnancy. The art of growing old is the art of being regarded by the oncoming generations as a support and not as an obstacle, as a confidant and not as a rival.

There is much to be said about retirement. It kills many men. Those are the ones who did not know how to prepare for it. For the man who has retained his curiosity intact, retirement can be the most delightful period of his life. What is needed in order to make retirement enjoyable? One must be aware of the emptiness of public renown and desire the peace of obscurity; one must maintain the wish to understand and to learn; one must maintain in his village, his house, or his garden, some limited personal activity. Having spent all his time to his public activities, the wise man now devotes himself entirely to his personal affairs and cultural development. This will be easier for him if he has been able to interest himself in poetry and the beauty of nature, even during his busiest years. For myself, I cannot imagine a more beautiful old age than one spent in the country, not far from a city, where I could reread and annotate some books I have loved very much. "The mind," says Montaigne, "must thrive upon old age as the mistletoe upon a dead oak." The dead ones continue to be our friends, whom death has been powerless to separate from us. Great writers are immortal companions who can embellish our old age as they enchanted our young days. Music too, is an extraordinarily faithful friend. To those who have lost their faith in human feelings, music offers a refuge with admirable worlds recreated every day. One evening at the opera not long ago, after a particularly sublime rendition of Beethoven's *Seventh Symphony*, I watched the faces of the people around me. Everyone, both young and old, seemed to be transported with enthusiasm and delight. I am sure there were embittered, weary, and tired souls among them, but these were equally enchanted. Carried away by the waves of sound, caressed by the ocean dew of the melodic themes, warmed and freed by the flame of the composer's genius, they abandoned themselves to beatitude, regardless of age and pain, experiencing an almost divine joy; I then understood those great men of old times who arrange to die while listening to the music they had loved most.

"Life is joyous," says Pascal, "when it begins with love and ends with ambition." It will be even happier if, after all ambition has been satisfied or overcome, it ends in serenity. Thus, having passed the line of shadow at fifty, ten or twenty years later there is a line of light a man may cross. The first assaults of old age seemed painful to him. He suffered when he saw that the times which he had thought to be his own were given over to new thoughts and new personalities. Now, on the contrary, he enjoys a peaceful happiness by remaining an alert and a disinterested spectator of the times that are no longer his. The tranquillity in his face, and the humorous and frank clarity of his gaze, vividly portray the state of his soul. No, it is not true that old age is a hell above whose gate must be written: "Abandon all hope, ye who enter here." We have analyzed the reasons for despair which an old man believes he has, and we have shown that none of them is irremediable. Old age, we say, does it deprive us of strength? Well, this is a matter of health rather than age; there are vigorous old ones, and young ones who are weak and sluggish. Does old age deprive us of pleasures? Well, it has its own, more delicious and loved when we know they are short-lived. Does old age deny us of activity? Well, sometimes old ones work, lead, and govern better than young ones. Does old age deprive us of friends? Well, on the contrary, a worthy old age surrounds us with many friends. And finally, does old age fear death? Well, this is the fear that faith and philosophy cure the best.

7. — THE ART OF DYING

> "We know not whether death be good
> But life at least will not be.
> Men will stand saddening as we stood,
> Watch the same fields and skies as we.
> And the same sea.
>
>   Swinburne.

There are two good ways of dying: the way of the Epicurean who believes that death is nothing, and the way of the Christian who believes that it is everything. "Accustom thyself," says Epicurus, "to the idea that death is nothing that relates to us; for good and evil consist in nothing but our perception of them and death is the loss of all perception. The realization that death is nothing is one of the joys of mortal life . . . For there is nothing truly horrible in life for him who really understands that there is nothing after it has ended. . . Death does not exist, because while we exist there is not death, and when there is death we do not exist." The Christian philosopher does not fear death, for he regards it merely as a transition, after which he is confident of finding those he has loved and of enjoying an existence infinitely more satisfying than his earthly years.

It is hardly surprising that saints and heroes should die well. But without reaching the borders of the sublime, good workers die noble deaths while doing their work to the end. "Professional" deaths have their own glory. One remembers the agonies of Balzac and of Proust, surrounded by the characters they had created, one calling the doctor Bianchon, and the other kept scribbling the name of Forcheville. Do you know the last words of Father Bouhours, the grammarian? "I am going to die, or I will die, we can say it either way." Charles II of England died like a king and a like a gentleman: "I have taken an unbelievably long time to die; I hope you will forgive me." Richelieu, the minister, was asked "Do you forgive your enemies?" He replied: "I have none save those of the State." Corot, the painter, expressed: "I sincerely hope, with all my heart, that I would be able to paint in heaven." Chopin, the musician, said: "Play Mozart in memory of me." Napoleon, the leader: "France. . . army . . . head of the army." Cuvier, the anatomist: "The head is inserted." Lacépède, the naturalist: "I will join Buffon." Madame Louise, the courtesan: "To Paradise! Quickly, quickly, to the big gallop."

Occasionally a man is so profoundly absorbed by his profession that it survives him, as it were. Halle, the philosopher, who was also a doctor, took his own pulses up to the last. "My friend," he said to one of his colleagues, "the artery has stopped beating." These were his last words. Lagny, the mathematician, at the beginning of the eighteenth century published a "completely new" and abridged method for extracting square and cube roots. When he was dying, he appeared to be unconscious and no longer recognized his friends. Someone leaned over him and said: "Lagny, what is the square of twelve?" Lagny answered: "One hundred and forty four." He was dead.

"If I were a composer of books," wrote Montaigne, "I would publish an annotated compendium of various kinds of deaths." Two English writers[1] have published the book that Montaigne desired. After finishing this curious reading, one experiences a feeling of respect for human values. There is little cowardice in its pages. "To die, to sleep, nothing else . . . But in this sleep of death, what dreams may come?" Even if Hamlet's terrible question remains unanswered, it is useful to know that kings, artists or poor human beings in every walk of life, have courageously asked it.

---

[1]Birrel and Lucas.

8. — AN OPEN LETTER TO THE YOUTH

"Here is a smile to those who loved me,
And a Sigh to those who hate;
And whatever sky's above me,
Here's a heart for every fate."

Byron.

You are beginning life during difficult times. Throughout history there have been rising tides which have taken even the weakest swimmers to success. Your generation swims against the current of a stormy sea. It is hard. In a short while you will feel suffocated; you will feel desperate to reach the shore. Rest assured. Before you, there have been others who have faced waves just as high and they were not sunken. With skill and courage you will survive until the next bonanza.

Once you have succeeded, do not forget that human victories are merely partial and temporary. Nothing in the affairs of this world is solved forever. There is no triumph which determines the long-term occurrences. No treaty can settle the relationships among nations, nor their geographical borders, in the distant future. No revolution can establish an eternally joyous society. Avoid the hope that a man, or a generation, will have the right to enjoy extravagant benefits once they have fulfilled his duty. The stage of life only ends at dusk.

Do not believe that human nature may be transformed simply because a doctrine, a race, or a class has succeeded over the others. Man is a beast who is beginning to walk straight thanks to philosophers and priests, and tamed by ceremonies and rituals. To renounce the beliefs and habits time has tested would mean to throw him into savagery. The only true progress is that achieved by changes in our customs. Those changes will not last unless they occur slowly.

Do not hurry. Fortune and renown that happen in an instant, in an instant will die. I wish you obstacles and battles. Battles will harden you. At about fifty or sixty years of age you will have acquired the vigorous and strong appearance of those old shoreline-rocks beaten by storms. The hostile world will have sculpted you. You will be characters, but you will also have character and the waves of public opinion will make you laugh. When one is young, everything seems terrible; the first obstacles encountered are taken as offenses. Human evilness terrifies us. Seek an inner shelter against the cruelty of people and things. Every man can build, in the inner recesses of his consciousness, a refuge that defies the heaviest attacks and the most poisoned words. What can a soul in peace with itself be afraid of? No amount of persecution or calumny can invalidate the support that this inner peace gives to the deepest thoughts.

Take love seriously, not tragically. In your adolescence you will be hurt by the futility of women, for their flirting, for their lies, for their cruelty. Tell yourself that those aspects of their behavior, although very real, are superficial. When observing women, think about the ocean, whose surface is constantly changing; but for those who approach and get to know the ocean, it is a faithful friend. Behind the tight rows of women too easily offered, search for those virtuous souls who hesitate before revealing their sweetness and before giving their confidence. Pledge fidelity whole heartedly to the one who seems worthy. Do not envy Don Juan; I have known him very well; he was the most unhappy, the most restless, the weakest amongst humans.

Be constant and steady. I know that when things do not work well one feels the urge to throw away the hammer after missing the mark, to start a new relationship with another woman, with other friends, under different skies. Do not yield to this apparent easiness. In some extreme cases it may occur that agonizing unhappiness makes it absolutely necessary to start anew; but for the majority of us it is better to take any possible advantage of what one already has. To age and to die amongst those with whom one has grown and struggled is a glorious destiny.

Finally, be modest and bold. To love, to think, to work, and to lead are all difficult tasks, and during the course o1f your earthly existence you will not accomplish any of them as perfectly as you dreamed it during your adolescence. But regardless of how difficult they seem, they are not by any means impossible. Before you, innumerable generations of men have accomplished them and, wisely or poorly, those men journeyed through the narrow zone of the light of life, between two deserts of shadows. What are you afraid of? The paper is limited, and the public is mortal even as you are.

IT IS IN YOUR HANDS:
EMOTIONAL FREEDOM TECHNIQUE

The Power to Eliminate Stress, Anxiety, and All Negative Emotions

Sobeida Salomon, Ph.D.

An introduction to a revolutionary psychological therapeutic method called Emotional Freedom Technique (EFT), which places in the hands of the user the power to eliminate all negative emotions, including stress, anxiety, fears, phobias, past traumas, substance abuse, and all addictions. With EFT the user no longer has to go through months of expensive, and usually ineffective, conventional "talk therapies." In a matter of minutes, anyone can be free from any negative emotional or psychological difficulty. It is simple, effective, and most importantly, it is free! EFT accesses the body's energy meridian system and releases the negative energy attached to a negative emotion. All one needs to do is to learn a series of meridian end points in the body, how to use the hands to tap on these points for a few minutes, and the ability to concentrate and feel a particular negative emotion one wants to eliminate. **IT IS IN YOUR HANDS** is written in a simple style, with many practical exercises, case studies to treat specific negative emotions, and illustrations designed to gradually develop and apply the principles.

About the Author: Dr. Sobeida Salomon is a sociologist and an expert in adult education and counseling. She has a Ph.D. from the University of Kentucky and a M.Sc. from Guelph University (Canada). She has many years of international experience in counseling, substance abuse prevention, and gender/cultural issues. She has worked with local and state governments, universities, and nonprofit organizations. Dr. Salomon has conducted qualitative research in the area of gender development, smoking cessation, and health promotion.

Published by:
SpiralPress
1217 Charter Lane
Ambler, PA 19002
E-mail: hydroscience@earthlink.net
http://home.earthlink.net/~hydroscience

THE THREE SPIRITS

Applications of Huna to Health, Prosperity, and Personal Growth

Sergio E. Serrano, Ph.D.

Sergio E. Serrano, Ph.D.

"If you are not using Huna, you are working too hard." Max Freedom Long, author of The Secret Science Behind Miracles

Huna means "secret" in the Hawaiian language. It refers to the coded knowledge of the ancient Kahunas, who were known for healing the sick, controlling the weather, walking over hot lava, and predicting and changing the future. You can use the principles of Huna to improve your health, better your finances, increase wealth, acquire material possessions you desire, achieve personal and professional objectives, enrich your relationship with others, and enhance the overall quality of life. Perhaps you have used visualization before, but do not know why sometimes it does not work. Know the forces and meet the entities of your mind that control the art of mental creation. Develop and use the skills necessary to effectively and efficiently achieve your desires. Huna techniques are combined with Thought Field Therapy (TFT) and Emotional Freedom Techniques (EFT). TFT/EFT methods are based on energy therapies similar to acupuncture. They have been shown to effectively remove deep psychological fixations, complexes, fears, anxiety, phobias, and negative emotions, without the need of expensive "talk therapies." Written in a simple style, the book includes many practical exercises and illustrations designed to gradually develop and apply the principles.

About the Author: Dr. Sergio E. Serrano is an engineer, scientist, and university professor. He is an example of the wave of scientists increasingly interested in studying psychic phenomena from a rigorous point of view.

Published by:
SpiralPress
1217 Charter Lane
Ambler, PA 19002
E-mail: hydroscience@earthlink.net
http://home.earthlink.net/~hydroscience

NOTES: